CERTITUDES

Nihil obstat

Arthur J. Scanlan, S.T.D.,
Censor Librorum.

Imprimatur

✠ Patrick Cardinal Hayes
Archbishop, New York.

New York July 26, 1927

CERTITUDES

BY

SISTER M. ELEANORE, C.S.C., Ph.D.

DEAN OF ENGLISH, SAINT MARY'S COLLEGE,
NOTRE DAME, INDIANA

Essay Index Reprint Series

BOOKS FOR LIBRARIES PRESS

FREEPORT, NEW YORK

First Published 1927
Reprinted 1968

LIBRARY OF CONGRESS CATALOG CARD NUMBER:
68-16956

PRINTED IN THE UNITED STATES OF AMERICA

TO
MY BROTHER AND SISTER

Grateful acknowledgment is made to the editors of the magazines in which these essays originally appeared for permission to reprint them in this collection.

SISTER M. ELEANORE.

CONTENTS

I. THE NEW POETRY

SUBJECT MATTER

THERE is much wasting of words nowadays in contentious discourses concerning the subject matter of poetry. The conservative poets hold fast to the idea that poetry should concern itself only with matter which is beautiful and ennobling in itself. The radicals declare that anything whatsoever, the more commonplace the better, is matter for poetry. On reading the table of contents in Marguerite Wilkinson's *New Voices* one will discover poems grouped under the terms democracy, patriotism, love, religion, nature, personality, and children. It seems to me these are the same old themes that have been in use as long as there has been poetry. Those who do not like the matter of the new poetry might say that the radical poets have taken from poetry the God of the Christian and substituted for Him the god of the Freudian complex. But any such wholesale condemnation of even the radicals would be obviously unjust. For my part I never enjoy poetry born in sewers, whether in the subterranean channels of the cities or in the channels of the subconscious mind. And, getting away from the subnormal, I shall always think that only Robert Burns would have dared to write a poem to the small traveler on the bonnet of the unfortunate lady who sat in front of him at church. He should have been saying his prayers, anyway.

When we talk of the subject matter of poetry we necessarily introduce the question of art. The definitions of art are legion. Two I like are "inspired utility" and "the concrete embodiment of a beautiful ideal." Symbolic art portrays the significance of spiritual beauty. Purely imitative art is the substitution of one sense medium for another. Almost every one admits that art is an attempt to embody the beautiful, that it deals with the beautiful as found in the world of sense. From this we may establish the theory that the subject matter of poetry is beauty, and that the theme of the individual poem is some individual beautiful thing. Now, let us investigate the nature of the beautiful, and then we shall be prepared to understand and criticize the new poetry in terms of beauty and its expression.

In the *Manual of Scholastic Philosophy* Cardinal Mercier states, after the teaching of St.

Thomas, that beauty, as all other concepts, is to be considered as derived from experience. Experience teaches that beauty gives a pleasure which is different from the pleasure given by the possession of the good or by the knowledge of the true and that this pleasure is based on knowledge derived by contemplation. This means that the perception of the beautiful does not engender a desire for a more exclusive possession of the beautiful, because the love of the beautiful is due not to its usefulness but to its beauty. "The beautiful is that which when seen gives pleasure." The beautiful comes to us only through the higher senses of sight and hearing. Hence, that may be called beautiful whose apprehension gives a certain pleasure to the intellect when it is stimulated by the message from the higher senses and gets the idea behind the sense perception for contemplation. Great art lives because the first contemplation of it does not exhaust its capacity to give pleasure, that is, the senses can bring from it ever new pleasure to the mind.

Beauty requires, however, certain responses from the one who contemplates it: an active intelligence, and the dispositions constituting good taste. Love of the beautiful springs from intellectual cognition and hence is of a spiritual nature. To appeal to the senses beauty resides necessarily in some object. In order that an object may be beautiful, it must have integrity, clarity, and proportion. A thing to be truly beautiful must be also good and true, though beauty is not synonymous with truth and goodness, for a thing may be good and true without being beautiful.

In our criticism of the new poetry there are two points to be considered: its art as expressing the ideals of the new poets, and our own abilities to appreciate it. To form a fair judgment of a poem we must ask ourselves certain questions. Does it give a pleasure in which the mind can rest? Is this pleasure derived from the contemplation of beauty embodied in the poem? Has the poem the qualities necessary to beauty? Have we the sympathies in taste necessary to appreciate the poem?

After this array of questions I proceed diffidently. Personally I like some of the new poets and their poems better than some of the old ones, but I think most of them are inclined to ignore what I consider the chief business of the poet, that is, to discover the permanent truth behind facts. The new poets introduce too much of the trivial, the sordid, and the passing into their poetry; but poetry filled with such substance does not live. A Robert Burns did lift a field mouse into poetry by appealing to pity, a most fleeting emotion, but we have kept the poem only because we love its author. As for Wordsworth, I can never understand how one who could pen that glorious line, "Whose dwelling is the light of setting suns," could write that stupidly cruel and inexcusable poem "The Idiot Boy." Life is filled with tragedies that crush the spirit of man as a steam roller can crush his body. We see them in the suffering faces of others if we do manage to escape them ourselves. Why, then, should we multiply them in poetry? Let the scientist deal with the perverted and the subnormal, let the novelist draw them for us if he feels that by doing so he can accomplish good, but let poetry be devoted to our joy and our soul's peace.

There are two poetic exhibits of life and nature, the universal and the particular. For the universal we may go to the Bible, to Homer, to the Attic dramatists, to Dante, and to Shakespeare. For the particular we may study Tennyson, Browning, Bryant, and many others. Poetic truth is both idealistic and realistic. The poet must be a realist in knowledge and an idealist in interpretation of his knowledge. He must observe truth of ethical import. Enduring poetry makes for good, though the poet must not preach. His mission is to teach us the true and beautiful in life, "to redeem from decay the visitations of the divinity" in us, to lift our minds and hearts to a plane of vision that will make us see lesser things ennobled and beautified by faith and hope. What, then, shall we say of poets who insist upon seeing only the exteriors of things and drawing pictures of them, who do not think straight in matters of faith and morals, whose only appeal to us is sense appeal, or, at least, an emotional appeal with no element of spiritual control?

It would be altogether unfair to condemn the new poetry as a whole just because some of the radical poets have ruled out the spiritual from the universe and have revolted from the "interiority of the cosmic poet." Many of the imagist poets, when they have escaped from their theories, have given us glorious metaphors. What, after all, are Thompson's "Hound of Heaven" and *"Lilium Regis"* but imagist poetry? And yet, there never was a more "interior" poet than Thompson. So, though we shudder at the violation of the decent silence that shrouds the weaknesses of the dead in Masters' *Spoon River Anthology*, though we discern with disgust the morbid sex appeal beneath the fair cloak of words in far too much of the modern poetry, though we regret the irreligious tendencies that could give birth to Hardy's "God's Funeral" and "A Plaint to Man," though we believe that poetry has been degraded by her forced association with sewers and ash cans and stockyards, we must, nevertheless, look for the golden wheat among the rotting chaff, because it is there. We must admit the freshness and vigor of much of the new poetry. If we who love poetry as "the lesser sister and helpmate of the Church" reject her now because her radiant robes are stained with the mud of materialism, we need to remember Francis Thompson's warning, "If you have no room for her beneath the wings of the Holy One, there is place for her beneath the webs of the Evil One. . . . Suffer her to wanton, suffer her to play, so she play around the foot of the Cross!" Condemn some of the radicals we must, but we must admit as well that many of the new poets do dream dreams and see visions of beauty and have been able to catch the lovely fugitive within the network of golden song. And for them, we who love poetry have reason to give thanks.

DICTION

If the insurgents in verse-making have not done anything else for us they have at least startled us from our self-sufficiency in regard to the diction of poetry. In the manner of Paul Verlaine they tell us brutally to "take eloquence and wring its neck." Then William Butler Yeats adds that we must "strip away everything that is artificial," by which he means that we must say "fish" instead of "ocean's scaly breed," "pipe" instead of "the short tube that fumes beneath the nose," "boot," instead of "the shining leather that encases the limb," and "wind" instead of "trembling zephyr." Before they began thus teaching, Walt Whitman did these two things. In the midst of the confusion poor Wordsworth's ghost has been trying to make himself heard to tell us that in two prefaces written long ago he said what all the *vers-librists* are saying. Be this as it may, we who cling to the old traditions must realize that dead are the days of "fleecy cloudlets," "mysteries strange of spring the vernal," "memoried moods," "azure domes," and the like.

In getting away from stereotyped phrases the new poets have done well. They insist that things be presented in concrete terms which will furnish images to the eye and sounds to the ear, that diction be not vague and abstract but simple, sincere, and individual, and that the poet use the language of everyday speech. The extremists of course carry their efforts too far. In their wish to create vivid images they use too many color words, such as saffron and mauve, with the result that the mind's eye sees pictures rivaling the most flamboyant comic section. Some of the new poems make me think of savages who wear the least possible amount of clothes and the greatest possible amount of paint.

There are fashions in literary diction just as in clothes, and there is usually something in each succeeding fashion to recommend it. In the eighteenth century an ocean of high-sounding words swept over poetry. A man was not blind in one eye in those days; rather, "to one the fates the visual ray deny." One did not pour coffee; instead, "from silver spouts the grateful liquors glide." Francis Fawkes even laid hands on the Bible and poetized it in a manner that is positively pathetic. No wonder that Wordsworth reacted from this poetic style and bade poets choose their subjects from common things and make "a selection of language really used by men." His theory was fine and sound, but his application of it to his own poetry was extreme and too often led him into the trivial. When he let genius and not theory be his guide he wrote as one in a vision, with the simplicity of diction that comes from abundance of vocabulary. Wordsworth's school provoked the inevitable reaction, and in the nineteenth century came the romanticists with their sumptuous diction to lead poetry into "murmurous glooms" and "labyrinthine, verdurous deeps." And now, in the twentieth century, come the insurgents to preach again the "language of common speech."

In regard to poetic diction there are three special points to be considered: Is there essential difference betwcen the dictions of prose and poetry? Which are the respective values of Anglo-Saxon and Latin words? What is poetry to do with archaisms and neologisms? I believe there is no essential difference between the dictions of prose and poetry. There is just the same accidental difference that exists in all the varied uses of language, the difference, for example, that there is between the dictions of the pulpit and of the platform. Some critics and poets teach that the words of prose, especially scientific prose, are chosen for their denotative value whereas the words of poetry are chosen for their connotative value. There is no doubt that some words are more easily assimilated by poetry than others, such words as sun, moon, stars, winds, home, love, joy, and sorrow. These words, as Joubert says, "reverberate like the note of a well-tuned lyre, and always leave behind them a multitude of vibrations." Yet the most common and least connotative words when in poetic associations may touch the deepest chords in the human heart. Love is perhaps the most used and abused of poetic themes, and words often are lifted by it from the commonplace or are dragged in the mire. When Robert Burns wrote of the pain of parted lovers, he used the common words of everyday speech to convey his message of suffering:

> *Had we never lov'd sae kindly,*
> *Had we never lov'd sae blindly,*
> *Never met—or never parted,*
> *We had ne'er been broken-hearted.*

Somehow the vanity of regret in these lines appeals to me ever so much more than that in Miss Lowell's lines concerning a knight:

> *He will go about his business with an ineradi-*
> *   cable complaisance,*
> *Leaving his dead to rot, his women to weep and*
> *   regret, his sons to wax into his likeness.*

So, too, in the words "sae kindly" and "sae blindly" I can read more of the love of the soul (though of course not of the love of the body) than in these sentences by Miss Lowell:

> *He will lean above you, Scherezade, like September above an orchard of apples.*
> *He will fill you with the sweetness of spice-fed flames.*
> *Will you burn, Scherezade, as flowers burn in September sunlight?*

Miss Lowell has here accomplished the aim of the free-verse writer: to furnish images (I am tempted to say stimuli) to the senses, albeit most young women would find it difficult to imagine themselves as an orchard of apples. But I, of course, am hopelessly old-fashioned and stupidly literal and deplorably reticent. Still, I can but wonder modestly whether I am not correct in thinking that the fundamental thing in poetic diction is not so much the word itself as the use of it. Any word that is strong enough to be necessary to the context and that expresses the exact meaning of the poet is a poetic word. Here is an illustration of words used well by Florence Earle Coates:

If love were but a passing breath—
Wild love—which, as God knows, is sweet—
One might not make of life and death
A pillow for love's feet.

And Sara Teasdale, with the same exquisite simplicity of diction, writes:

There is a quiet at the heart of love
And I have pierced the pain and come to peace.

Both these poets have voiced the truth that pain, too often, is as the pursuing shadow of love. And here, as in all questions of literary character, I shall turn to the Bible as the final court of appeal. Where in all writings is there anything like these words from the Lover to His beloved? "Peace I leave with you, my peace I give unto you: not as the world giveth, do I give unto you. Let not your heart be troubled, nor let it be afraid." The new poets teach well when they bid us study the Bible.

It is easily evidenced that the words in our language of the greatest connotative power are of Saxon origin. Practically all the words relating to home and family are from the Saxon, and bring with them numberless emotional associations. Yet poetry would be hurt by the loss of such Latin words as "maternal," "silent," "remembrance." If we should take from Mrs. Meynell's poem, "The Shepherdess," its two Latin words, "maternal" and "circumspect," we should not be able to substitute their equals. Since the Saxon is no longer a spoken language it will have to gain its new words from other tongues. In regard to neologisms the only safe principle is that of intelligibility, for surely the prime requisite of poetry is to be understood. Some of our old poetic expressions are now ruled out as archaisms. We must not write "dost" and "e'er" and "'neath." Even the pronoun "thou," once the purest poetic gold, has become rusty with disuse.

Intelligibility is the one real test of words. Hence, let words be beautiful as they will; let them "shine around our simple earth with golden shadowings"; and let "every common thing they touch be exquisite with wings." But always let them bring the message of the poet into our hearts. The reason why I fail to appreciate the poetry of some of the insurgents is that I sometimes have to consult the dictionary several times during the reading of a poem. Justly humiliated by this admission, I yet wonder whether I am the only person who is forced to do so.

TECHNIQUE

Though the difference in technique between the old and the new poetry is to those not learned in the lore of the moderns as a rule simply the difference between poetry and prose, the new poets insist that they are writing poetry. Some of them are ready and willing to give reasons for the faith that is in them. They tell us, believing that such benighted folk need the information, that Oriental poetry, Hebrew poetry, and old Teutonic poetry have neither meter nor rhyme. Nor are we allowed to protest feebly that we are not writing Oriental or Hebrew or old Teutonic poetry, that we want simply to keep on writing poetry as English poets have been accustomed to write it. They tell us also that prose has its rhythm as well as poetry has its rhythm and that they have found the river into which the two streams flow. Thus have they come to freedom.

Formal verse is made by the welding of two rhythms: the metrical rhythm, and the rhythm of the phrasal overtone. It is possible, for example, to read in two ways these four lines from Thompson's *"Lilium Regis"*—that distilled essence of poetic beauty called an ecclesiastical ballad:

O Lily of the King! low lies thy silver wing,
And long has been the hour of thine unqueen-
ing;
And thy scent of Paradise on the night wind
spills its sighs,
Nor any take the secrets of its meaning.

First, one may read it by stressing the metrical beat of the iambics. Then, one may read it in phrases, with pauses between them. I defy any one thus to read those four lines aloud without a shiver at their exquisite music. In them is every pet aversion of the *vers-librists:* interlinear rhyme, meter, apostrophe, metaphor, alliteration, subjectivity. Now the flower of beauty in those lines is the lovely phrasal overtone playing in and out through the regular beat of the meter. Moreover, such poetry can stand up straight because it has a backbone made of rhyming words.

The free-verse writer recognizes that the phrasal overtone is the beautiful thing in poetry, and so he determines to make his verse only of phrasal overtones or, as he calls them, cadences. For the single melody playing in and out through the metrical beat as a singer's voice plays in and out through its orchestral accompaniment, now rising above it, now falling below it, now melting into it, but always leading and ruling it, the free-verse writer substitutes an erratic and unaccompanied soloist. Thus, he says, he has secured freedom. One would think he had, provided one had not read Miss Lowell's textbooks on the art of making free verse. But if one has read them one realizes sadly that making formal verse is but child's play as compared to making so-called free verse.

Before we investigate the rules of *vers-libre* let us weigh the worst charge made by the new poets against formal poetry. It is that formal verse writers are compelled to make use of inversions in order to make their words fit the meter. Look again at Thompson's lines. "Low lies thy silver wing." Rhetoricians tell us that even in prose we should place emphasis on the important word. The important word in that sentence is "low," and it has the most emphatic place among the five words. Rhetoric, not meter, determined its position, as that of the word "long" in the second line. There is no inversion in the third and fourth lines, unless "on the night wind" should follow "sighs." Write "thy silver wing lies low" and change the order in the third line, and you will not hurt the meter. Ah, but the rhyme, murmurs *Mr. Vers-Librist.* I surrender. To take the rhyme from those lines is just the same as to pull the tail from a peacock and ask him to be as beautiful as he was before the disaster.

Whereas the most radical new poets and the ungifted imitators of the real *vers-librists* do away with all rules and give us nothing but poor lines that cannot even be called prose by those of us who love it, the first-class poets of the movement do attempt to follow certain rules. These rules have been given their best expression by the late Amy Lowell in magazine articles and in her book, *Tendencies in Modern American Poetry.* But the free-verse movement antedates her. The Celtic renaissance, especially through the work of William Butler Yeats and John Synge, brought into English literature the simple, clear song of early Irish poets to show us that we were becoming stilted and artificial in much of our own singing. This was good. Walt Whitman came into popularity in France and won the French poets to experimentation. Their influence traveled in turn to Ireland, England, and America. In the meantime the Orient came to us from its long-closed gates to bring its imagery and symbolism. Edward Fitzgerald introduced the Persian poet Omar Khayyám among us; Rabindranath Tagore in later years wrote his Indian songs in our language; Japan and China brought their delicate, simple songs among us. All this has made us more cosmopolitan.

Imagery, symbolism, and rhythm are bound indissolubly together, says Miss Lowell. "The definition of *vers-libre* is: a vèrse form based on cadence. . . . To understand *vers-libre*, one must abandon all desire to find in it the even rhythm of metrical feet. One must allow the lines to flow as they will when read aloud by an intelligent reader." It is "the rhythm of the speaking voice with its necessity for breathing," not a metrical system, that governs free verse. Irreverently, I offer condolences to short-winded people who try to read "Patterns" as it should be read. "Free verse within its own law of cadence has no absolute rules; it would not be 'free' if it had." Now, what is cadence? "The unit of *vers- libre* is not the foot, the number of the syllables, the quantity, or the line. The unit is the strophe, which may be the whole poem, or may be only a part. Each strophe is a complete circle." The strophe, then, is a sort of time measure, such as the swing of a pendulum. One may illustrate by a circle round which a man travels within five minutes. He may walk, skip, run, loiter, and pause; the main thing is the five minutes.

Now I can read poetry to my own satisfaction
and with the perhaps unwarranted assumption
that I am intelligent, but if some one should time
me with a stop watch I should feel that my freedom had been interfered with. A rhyme word
here and there does not bother me in the least.
As for the quality of return, it is present in formal poetry, and it is free and varied in almost
every form of verse, except perhaps the heroic
couplet. Even here, if the *vers-librists* are correct
in their contention that thought and rhythm are
inextricably wedded, thought and rhythm do both
wait on the period at the end of the second line
as the return of the strophe. Now that I have
hopelessly tangled the issue, I hasten to conclude
that the point is: the free-verse writers want to
get the strophic rhythm away from the uniform
beat of metrical lines. We, like the strophe, halt-
ingly and by skips, have reasoned ourselves back
to our starting point by traveling in a circle.

Why this quest for freedom? The new poets
insist that they have a new way of seeing things
and that they are concerned "with man in his
proper relation to the universe, rather than as
the lord and master of it." Of course, if man is
not the master of the universe but is only a mate-

rial part of it, he certainly has no right to impose his feelings upon things about him. He should keep his poetry exterior and objective; he should not use details of thought or emotion that will alter his pictures; he must never indulge in generalities or abstractions. The gist of the reasoning is, it seems to me, that the poet must deal only in facts and never in the truths that are behind the facts. And so, though I like the freshness and individuality of much of the new poetry and its rhythms and its diction, I think it fails to be true poetry because it is not big enough to carry the burden of truth. If the only difference between new and old poetry is ease in writing, the new poets may have the palm. But ease of production is not the standard by which we judge a work of art. Freedom is true freedom only when it is exercised within restraint for a worthy purpose. License is not freedom.

As for the question of meter and rhyme as compared to unrhymed cadence, one's decision must be based largely on taste. If you happen to like to hear Galli-Curci sing "Home, Sweet Home" without her accompanist and with "holds" that only she dares to attempt, and I happen to like to hear her with her accompanist, shall we therefore condemn each other's taste? Then, too, if I happen to like some of the new rhythms so much that I use them in writing verses, you have no right to call me a poetical heretic, just because you think there is no poetry in them.

II. THE CATHOLIC SPIRIT IN LONGFELLOW

LAD in the garments of holiness, poetry runs along the high road to Paradise. When degraded from this eminent estate, she too often leads the way to the Inferno. It is, then, the beautiful business of the teacher of youth to cull the flowers of celestial song from the pages of the poets, and, by offering them to the children, thus direct their hearts to God. If the minds of the young are filled with lovely thoughts, there will be no room in them for ugly ones. Children like poetry naturally, and they learn its lessons readily. The more singsong its rhythm is and the more obvious its message, the better they like it. The singsong rhythm and the obviousness of much of the poetry of Henry Wadsworth Longfellow may be the reasons why he is the poet best beloved of children.

It is almost a truism that a poet turns Catholic when he writes religiously, and it certainly is true of Longfellow. James J. Treacy appropriately includes several passages from Longfellow's poetry in his anthology *Catholic Flowers*. Longfellow, though he falls short of true greatness, has justly been called the poet of the hearth and the home; and one might even go so far as to call him the poet of the Catholic home. His poems are chiefly meditative, impressive in their earnestness, seldom rising to the heights of passion, and often embodying or illustrating significant truths. In many ways they are a mirror of his blameless life. I have selected a few illustrations of the Catholic spirit in his poetry, not at all with the intention of exhausting the subject but only with the hope of inspiring others, especially other teachers of literature, to seek further for Catholicism in his writings and in the writings of other poets as well.

English literature is so largely by Protestant authors that we who teach it must search it painstakingly for the Catholic truths we would wish our students to learn and keep. It seems that if we are to teach literature at all we must, for the greater part, teach Protestant literature. Yet much of this supposedly Protestant literature, especially the literature of poetry, is in reality surprisingly Catholic in message and setting. Here is the almost puritanical Longfellow, for example, steeping himself in Dante, in Catholic ritual, in medieval monasticism, so as to write his "Christus"; here is he, descendant of those who taught that faith alone is sufficient, teaching that faith without good works is dead; here is he, kin to those who accuse us Catholics of adoring Mary, writing with understanding sympathy of the Incarnation; here is he, amid those who fear everything Romish, calling the Pope the bridge from earth to Heaven and creating priests and nuns who are ideals. Longfellow is only another evidence that poets must turn Catholic when they write of religious themes, for the simple reason that poetry itself is at its best the voice of truth.

The Catholic Church has always insisted upon the necessity of good works in addition to faith; particularly, in accord with our Lord's teachings, does she stress the value of the corporal works of mercy. The doctrine that faith without good works is dead is set forth in "The Legend Beautiful," an exquisite extract from the *Tales of a Wayside Inn,* one of the poet's most pretentious works. The monk, praying in contrition for his sins of indecision and asking the grace of greater self-denial, is vouchsafed the Vision of our Lord. Rapt in adoration he hears the bell which summons him to distribute alms to the poor at the convent gate; and though loath to leave the Master he goes to answer it. The poor have long been accustomed to alms refused or carelessly given, but on this day there seems to be something sacramental in the bread and wine dispensed to them. His duty done, the monk returns to his cell, questioning himself as to whether he would have adored our Lord had He come in beggarly guise instead of in splendor. Then he finds the Vision awaiting him, and he understands fully the words, "Hadst thou stayed, I must have fled!"

This legend is the most beautiful among the tales told by the guests of the inn. The characters introduced and described in this series of stories, which are molded together in an interesting framework of place, time, and circumstances, represent a high average of respectability. In the stories Longfellow seems to have dipped his pen a few times into the cloudy ink of prejudice. "Torquemada" is a perversion of truth, unreliable in its authority and its misunderstanding of the purpose and administration of the Inquisition. "The Cobbler of Hagenau" has in it a thorough misconception of indulgences. Yet these are tales in character with their authors in the group gathered together by the poet. Longfellow might be criticized also from the Catholic point of view for attempting to poetize about the unpoetical Martin Luther and for writing out his mouthings against the Church. Yet here again, doubtless, he is simply allowing the apostate priest to speak in character.

Everybody knows the tale of "King Robert of Sicily," with its thoroughly Catholic setting and its theme, *"Deposuit potentes de sede, et exaltavit humiles";* and any child in the world will love it and learn its lesson. In "The Nun of Nidaros," by far the best part of "The Saga of King Olaf," we find the teaching that sorrow is necessary in life's weary journey, and therefore should be sweetened by resignation and hope and childlike trust in God.

These are only a few of the tales, and yet there is much Catholicity already. Of course there is a generous measure of the anti-Catholic as well, but that is to be expected. Longfellow gives us much less reason to quarrel with him in the "Christus," which dominated his whole literary life. The Catholic heart always looks for our Lady when our Lord is portrayed. The author fails to give us all we desire in the rich and artistically arranged narrative "The Divine Tragedy" from the "Christus," and yet his one mention of Mary in "The Marriage in Cana" brings her sweetly close. Longfellow keeps to the simple Biblical manner in relating the incidents of Christ's first miracle. In the second part of the poem "The Golden Legend" there is a passage uttered by Prince Henry on his entrance into Italy which conveys perfectly the Catholic idea of the Blessed Virgin's power with God and her willing intercession for her children. He concludes by saying that if the Catholic faith had given nothing more than Mary, it would have proved itself higher and truer than all the creeds the world has known. And he does not fail us in his story of the Incarnation. This work as a whole, in setting forth an ideal Catholic character in little Elsie and in showing the ultimate triumph of good over evil, is thoroughly Catholic. This, despite the wine-bibbing monks in the convent of Hirschau, for, after their revelry in which Lucifer participated, they were sent in disgrace to take the discipline.

The "Christus" is Longfellow's supreme effort, and it is very much worth while. There is nothing lacking in his treatment of St. Peter as head of the apostles and cornerstone of the Church. The introduction to "A Covered Bridge at Lucerne" is a remarkable conception for a non-Catholic, in its description of the Pope as "the chief builder and architect of the invisible bridge that

leads from earth to Heaven." In this poem Longfellow has caught the spirit of Holy Mother
Church. There is a peculiar dramatic contrast
in the ceremonies and liturgical phrases by which
the Church celebrates her joyful mysteries, such
as Christmas, Easter, and our Lady's feasts, and
in those by which she shrouds in sorrow Good
Friday and the burial service. Longfellow has
imitated this contrast in the framework that he
weaves about "The Marriage in Cana" with the
rapturous music of the Canticle of Canticles and
in the deathbed scene at Jairus' home with the
heartbreaking minor strains of the minstrels and
mourners. One might go on almost endlessly to
point out the Catholic spirit in the first two
parts of the "Christus," but I shall note only one
more selection that embodies this spirit. It is the
story of Bartimeus. Blind since the birth of his
child, he is healed by Christus and in human way
turns first to the loved Chilion and then to God.
He begs God's pardon for this offense, reminding
Him that He is Himself a Father and therefore
can understand. There is nothing of the Puritan
in this idea of God. It is sweetly Catholic.

Longfellow goes astray in "The Demoniac of
Gadara" by stating that numberless evil spirits,
including Cain and Belshazzar, had possession

of the unfortunate demoniac. These are discarnate souls, and as such cannot enter human bodies. Despite this and other errors, however, the whole poem is Catholic in tone and setting.

In the American epic, "Hiawatha," Longfellow gives us a true type of the priesthood in the Black-Robe Chief. In "Evangeline" he paints the Sister of Mercy as she really is, one who lives for others and follows meekly with reverent steps the sacred feet of Christ. Many other shorter poems also show the Catholic spirit in Longfellow's poetry.

One can but wonder that this singer of songs who understood the message of the Angel Gabriel to the Blessed Virgin, who could leave his burdens behind the cathedral door where "the eternal ages watch and wait," who seems to have been directed by the great principles of the moral law, who knew what St. Peter means to the true Church of Christ, who entered into the meaning of the functions of the priesthood, and who found no difficulty in the consecration of women to the religious life—all stumbling-blocks to the ordinary Protestant—one can but wonder that he was not moved to go further and pronounce his "credo" in the whole of Catholicism. Perhaps he is only another illustration that the poet, as well as the prophet, often sings of truths which he does not fully understand. Perhaps the "fine frenzy" of inspiration is not altogether a myth. Be that as it may, much of Longfellow's poetry belongs to our Catholic children as their right.

III. THE ALLEGED PESSIMISM
OF THE AMERICAN NOVEL

THE contemporary novel, particularly in America, is a pitiable hypochondriac. Poor old human nature, prey to divers ills, sits amid the novelists as Job sat among his comforters, who crying out weep and rending their garments sprinkle dust upon their heads—and into our eyes. "Woe, woe, and more woe," the theme of the old Greek drama in its tragic vein, is also the theme of the modern realistic novel. Pessimism is the literary style nowadays, and our young writers prefer death to unstylishness. The need of the day, especially in the United States, is for somebody with a hearty laugh, big and contagious enough to echo throughout the world—the Stephen Leacock of the *Nonsense Novels* magnified to the gigantic stature of a Dr. Samuel Johnson and developed to the sympathetic humor of a Fielding.

We have as a reading public gone back to the golden days of the immortal Richardson and the notorious Sterne, when unashamed tears from a sublime despair over human woe streamed from the eyes of Rousseau as he sat in delicious misery above Lake Geneva and from the mountain height taught his naturalized Gospel. In those days it was the custom for families to assemble and listen to one member while he read aloud some interminable novel of the year, and, when an especially harrowing passage was finished, to retire into separate chambers to weep. In these days when there is no place like home—to get away from, it seems—it would require a real exercise of the imagination to picture such a family group. Hearts were indeed worn upon sleeves in those times; and they were simply riddled by the sob-laden novel. Then along came Fielding with his *Joseph Andrews,* and the poor sniffling readers sat up, wiped their eyes, gasped, chuckled, and guffawed.

The history of the novel portrays the fact that reactions to extremes are inevitable. When Horace Walpole wrote the first of the Gothic romances that kept the reader's hair on end for two decades, he was preparing the way for Jane Austen's immortal burlesque, *Northanger Abbey.* This courageous, wholesome woman took the Gothic story from haunted towers, gruesome tombs, and weird stairways, aired it in the sunlight of her clean-hearted genius, and in its stead gave the novel of manners to a world which has loved her ever since. Cervantes ruined the Spanish romance of chivalry by his *Don Quixote*. It is high time for a reaction from the pessimism of contemporary fiction. We have novels of the "glad" variety and of the "if winter comes" ending, which fairly deluge us in the hopelessness of existing affairs and then bid us be brave and noble and look for rainbows and silver linings and all that. These are well enough in their way and will do some persons good; but what we Americans, above all peoples in the world, need is somebody who can make us see that we have no reason to be pessimistic, somebody who can make us laugh at ourselves, somebody who can make us understand that we take even our amusements in a spirit of bored martyrdom.

Laughter at self is most wholesome; self-pity is a dangerous moral disease. Our contemporary novelists are making us self-pitiful. We read the best sellers and then we can but conclude that marriage is a failure, that business men are all scoundrels, that every woman's virtue is fallible and every man is a beast, that dire want haunts the home of every workman, that justice always goes astray, and that if there should be a God He is asleep—in fact, that we are going fast to destruction. If all this be true we are indeed in a sorry way. If, however, the vast majority of us are sane, wholesome people who need neither jails nor asylums and who live in happy, comfortable homes, we have but little reason for pessimism. Why does the modern novelist harp everlastingly on the theme of woe? If he is sincere and understands life about him, most of us do need jails or asylums. To this the cynic will agree. If the novelist, however, really understands life about him in America then his pessimism can be but a literary pose. In the best sellers of the past two years one can hardly find a happy home, honor, sanity, kindness, chastity, or any other virtue most of us flatter ourselves that we possess.

When we seek the reason for this pessimism in the American novel we are driven to consider it an attempt to imitate the pessimism of the Europeans. Our novelists, it seems, have given themselves to the aping of a point of view and a manner of expression, while they have not the perspective and the subject matter to which that point of view and that manner of expression belong. The American novel is neurotic; it is that most pitiable of all creatures, the hypochondriac. It is much better for the individual to be sick enough to need an operation than to have a fixed idea that there are numberless ailments in his afflicted body, no one of which can be brought to the attention of a doctor skilled sufficiently, so the victim judges, to diagnose it. The only cure for such a person is concentration on the facts that he can walk, that he can see, that he can hear, that he is in fact very much like the rest of humanity, and that the only road to health is healthful living and hard work. So, too, the American novel needs first of all a good laugh at itself and then an earnest concentration on the normal, wholesome material everywhere ready for use. In this way only can it rid itself of its alleged pessimism.

The term, alleged pessimism, needs an explanation. There are three kinds of pessimism, hopeless, hopeful, and alleged. Hopeless pessimism considers this the worst of possible worlds with no hope of betterment. Of this pessimism Thomas Hardy is a noteworthy exponent. His is the doctrine of fatalism, of a universe at war with man and controlled by an unconscious force, the Immanent Will. When Tess was swinging from the gallows he said that Justice was done and Time, the arch-satirist had his joke out with her. Yet Thomas Hardy is a native of well-fed, complacent England, wherein "life flows along like a song"; and one must consider his pessimism rather the result of sour and bewildered egoism than of sour and bewildered reaction to observation. Joseph Conrad, though agreeing with Hardy that the universe is at war with man, differs from Hardy in the conception of its power. Hardy holds that the "indifference" of the universe is "the incarnate principle of disaster" in its relation to man; nature overshadows man, threatens him, and finally crushes him. Hardy's pessimism comes from the conviction that nature is more powerful than man; he cannot realize that an individual may be utterly defeated and yet be unconquered. Conrad, on the other hand, believes that nature is not capable of malevolency; he considers it rather a moral negation. His pessimism is paradoxical—as pessimism in the normal mind must ever be. In his despair of the cosmos including man he believes in man at war with the cosmos. The human soul that sees nature as a chilling, frightful enigma of nothingness must turn to man for comfort. Therefore the mind and the will of man are Conrad's hero.

The novel *Victory* sets forth this dual philosophy of conflict between man and man's world that includes himself. Axel Heyst, who falls into the uttermost decadence of pessimism, at length learns to put his faith in love which, though it is unholy because unsanctioned, leads him in the end to see that life is good if one can but trust in it. If such an evil as suicide could be artistic, one might say that Heyst's suicide when Lena's death has deprived him of the one human being in whom he trusts is the only possible artistic ending to his story. Yet one wishes that the end of the novel had been the girl's weary but triumphant smile as she died to teach him the lesson of faith in love and life. Joseph Conrad's pessimism has a note of hope in it, the recognition of the fact that a man may be utterly defeated and yet be unconquered. His is surely a pessimism born of his country, Poland, the crucified but the indomitable; but the son has not the greatness of his Catholic motherland. Poland, like Ireland, is brave because she has undying faith in God's justice. Conrad was a Catholic and his Catholicism forced him, perhaps unconsciously, into his recognition of the freedom of the human will to triumph over tragic circumstances. He failed, however, to introduce the essential doctrine of Catholic hopefulness in the eternal Justice that will right all wrongs. Axel Heyst dies in despair, when he might have been exalted to a life dedicated to hope of immortal happiness.

Russian literature has given us many examples of these two kinds of pessimism, because Russia has reason for being pessimistic. Of all peoples in the world the Russians have a history that is one long and awful tragedy. The gigantic Dostoevski, who understands the Catholic doctrine that the supreme exercise of the human will is an act of submission to God's will when rebellion would be the easier part because of apparently unconquerable difficulties in the way of unquestioning submission, has taught to the modern world the tragedy that is Russia; but he has not taught it by means of unrelieved pessimism. Provided that one keeps faith in the spirit of man and its Phœnix-like power to rise from the ashes of material ruin and even spiritual disaster to the heights of unquestioning trust in the providence of God, there is some excuse for pessimism when one lives in the midst of suffering; and therefore the pessimism of the Russians and the Poles may be justified. It is as night with a candle gleaming through the darkness, the candle being the indomitable will of man, held in utter abeyance to the will of God.

Set over against the genuine and rather well-founded pessimism of these European novelists is the alleged pessimism of the American fiction writers. It is fashionable nowadays among the young people of America to wear an expression of profound world-weariness, born of the conviction that things simply could not be worse than they are. If De Quincey's essay on "Murder, Considered as One of the Fine Arts" and Stevenson's "Suicide Club" were not open to the charge of satiric levity, they should be popular as spiritual reading, especially among our young college students. As a nation we have been appalled at the number of suicides among college students during the past months. We are, moreover, being literally deluged by a stream of pessimistic and lachrymose fiction. It is natural to seek the reason for such morbidity in the American novel of to-day, since most of us believe that one of the important functions of the novel is the reflection of life. Are we, indeed, in such a sorry state of ill-being?

America is a country of small towns, and therefore many of our critics hailed *Main Street* as *the* American novel—as if there could be an American novel, a novel big enough to embrace the lumber camps, the mining towns, the ranches, the plantations, the oil fields, the manufacturing districts, the upper and lower Fifth Avenues, the fruit farms, the various dialects, the labor problems, the religious differences, the woman question, and all the other things that are seething in the great melting pot. There is, moreover, the question whether *Main Street* gives a true and adequate picture of the midwestern town or gives merely a discontented woman's picture of the life and people there as she saw them. Granted that she is but the mouthpiece of Sinclair Lewis, the question remains as to the truthfulness of the book. The heroine was a square peg in a round hole, and yet she could not understand that the hole might be no more blameworthy and no less uncomfortable than the peg. She saw only the vulgar and the tiresome in Gopher Prairie, not realizing that there were beautiful things in it as well.

In Gopher Prairie, as in all towns, there were honest men who toiled for their homes and the interests of their town; there were women who suffered and bore children and made homes for them; there were old people who were content to look back upon a good and useful life; there were little boys who knew the glorious dreams of a Napoleon as they pitched a team to victory on the baseball lot; there were dear little girls dreaming over their dollies of a home and babies fashioned in the airy manner of rainbows; and, finally, there was Dr. Kennicott himself with his devoted love for Carol and his simple grandeur in the practice of a profession that could steel him to perform a dreadful operation by a small light in a dingy, dark room. These are beautiful things, and they are as truly Gopher Prairie as the town drunkard, the fallen woman, and the lack of culture are Gopher Prairie; and it was the duty of the creator of life in this town to see the whole of his creation. Yet Sinclair Lewis in the person of Carol Kennicott missed all the beauties, a human and understandable failure but one that kept his novel from true greatness.

America is a country wherein many women enter the business world. One of these women became the heroine of an American novel, *Bread*, by Charles Norris, in which a home is ruined by the wife, who prefers her business career to the business of making a home. In this novel Norris attempted to do one of two things: either to portray an already existing evil of sufficient establishment and importance to merit widespread attention, or to point out an impending catastrophe to the American people; that is, he must have had one of these purposes in view if he was sincere in writing this novel that, whatever its faults, makes the reader reflect seriously on its problem. A novel similar to this in theme but English in setting is Hutchinson's *This Freedom;* and the contrast in its ending to the ending of *Bread* affords a further emphasis to the determined pessimism of the American novelist. The woman in *This Freedom* becomes the victim of her own selfishness as does the woman in *Bread* but attains to contentment at last, whereas her less fortunate sister in America is deprived of all consolation save the dubious comfort of hugging a cat. Hutchinson deluges us in woe and then by a sort of *deus ex machina* process turns on a rainbow at the end to satisfy our desire that they "live happily ever after." Hence, we are expected to smile through tears when we close *This Freedom* and sob abandonedly when we lay down *Bread*.

Humanity in America, if we may judge by our reading public, is just as sentimental, in the worst sense of the term, as it was in the days of Sterne. And what shall be our attitude toward the pessimistic pose of our young novelists, who remind us of Laura Spencer Portor's *Margaret*, "so bent, since the foundation of the world, on proving herself right and everybody else wrong . . . a very piece of humanity—humanity, the ancient, the amusing, the faulty, the pathetic, the endeared?" We wonder that thousands of happily married women and pampered girls—for, excepting teachers and professional literary men, the reading public is composed of women and girls—should read with delight the stories of these two women who wrecked their lives for business careers. The only explanation seems to be based on curiosity, for we all like to adventure into strange circumstances and meet people different from ourselves.

The question must be asked, Does the heroine of *Bread* typify American women? Undoubtedly there are many women such as she in America, but an investigation into divorce records reveals that we have much less to fear from the woman who goes into business than from the woman who goes into society. Wrecked homes are more numerous among the idle rich than among the working classes. One might almost revise the old saying nowadays to read: When wealth comes into the home contentment flies out the window. The world may weep over children given to the care of nurses while the mother goes out to play bridge; and yet one can rightly wonder whether the little ones would be better off under the care of such a mother. There is something wrong in a woman who prefers a dog to a child, who can listen to dry lectures on social uplift but cannot uplift the hearts of her children by teaching them to pray, for such a woman has without understanding sold her sacred birthright for less than a mess of pottage. There are many such women in this country, but happily they are at the pointed top of the pyramid of social life, whereas the broad base made up of the simple working classes stands firm. And we feel with Vernon Lee when, as she looked upon the snug homes for happy people in Werther's Wetzlar, she "half felt that *they* and all they stood for, might possess the dream-stuff quality we call romance" and that a story told of them might forever "echo and set our heart-strings vibrating to its tone." We agree with her that in every town and city of the world there are men and women who have loved and are loving "as deeply and sadly and radiantly" as any hero and heroine of fiction, "their lives, even if but for an instant, flushed into poetry by passion," and that they are the "strings, albeit often rusty and jangling, without which Genius, with howsoever a sweeping hand, cannot bring forth its music."

When the huge and genial Chesterton looked across the United States he saw a forest of small wooden houses with window lights shining like

stars through the darkness, and in them he found
reason for the "undefinable savour" of "old-fashioned American literature," which has in it the
"smell of growing things," the "smell of wood."
Is it not sad that because of the alleged pessimism
of our young novelists contemporary fiction has,
not the smell of growing things, but the smell of
decaying things, decaying virtue, decaying loves,
and decaying homes? Yet the little wooden
houses remain, and, as Kilmer wrote, they still
"put their loving wooden arms around a man and
his wife." Do these writers think they are giving
the public what it likes? A short time ago the
publishers of *Tom Sawyer* and *Huckleberry Finn*
manufactured fifty thousand copies of each of
these books to carry them through the coming
year. Two of the "best sellers" in the United
States are *Ben Hur* and *David Harum*. Though
every public library in this country has sets of
Dickens' works, somehow there are as many as
fifty editions of certain of his novels being manufactured every year. Contrast the lasting popularity of these books with the flash into popularity
and speedy oblivion of the "best sellers" of the
past twenty years. Naturally the young novelists
watch their contemporaries, study their methods
and themes, and then "go and do likewise," for

they reckon that the present income from Dickens'
books is of little material comfort to their author.
What a pity it is that more of our writers cannot adopt the improvident Lamb's blithe slogan,
"Hang posterity, I'll write for antiquity," and
thus win the popularity that counts. But they
reason instead, "I must have bread for the family." Gone are the days when a Goldsmith was
locked in his room by an irate landlady till Johnson sold one of his immortal pieces of literature;
gone are the days when genius was willing to labor
during twice seven years for its lady fame. They
who write nowadays tell us that America starves
all her dreamers of visions, forgetting that nations have always starved their visionaries. Men
are willing to give themselves as food for cannon
in the name of patriotism, but they are not willing
to spend their lives in teaching ideals to a needy
people. How many are the novels that teach
the sanctity of marriage to a country needing such
gospel as ours does? Granted that there is one
divorce for every ten marriages in certain districts of America, the proportion is, even yet, nine
to one; and the agitation throughout the country
to tighten up the laws shows that we realize the
danger threatening not only our family but our
national welfare as well. Here is opportunity

fore the American novel of to-day deserves the hard name hypochondriac. May the kindly fates who preside over the births of literary people send us a genius to be our doctor who, like the sought-after though universally hated dentist, may remind us that though one tooth is aching the other twenty-seven are behaving as normal teeth should. Then we shall understand that our "submerged tenth" is, after all, only a tenth; that not all marriages are failures even though an appreciable percentage of married persons are too selfish to be happy; that the greater number of homes have a real mother and lovable children in them; and even that we may without rank injustice call ourselves a Christian people. The times are ripe for a prophet who will fill up the valleys of despondency and level the hills of undue optimism and straighten the crooked paths of modern philosophy, in order that good old-fashioned faith in humanity may walk across the reading world.

IV. THE WHOLE TRUTH

THE modern novelists, with some few notable exceptions, fail to see the whole truth in life and the representation of life in fiction. Many of them believe with H. L. Mencken that the primary aim of the novel is "the representation of human beings at their follies and villainies." Truly, every one of us can bear shamed testimony to the fact that human beings have superabundant follies and villainies. On the other hand, every one of us can bear proud testimony to the fact that human beings have also innumerable virtues. Any one who professes to tell us the truth about life must show both these facts. I grant that many of us are locked in jails and asylums and that many more of us might well be locked up. I grant that many of us could not better become our lives than by amending them. But I acclaim with trumpets that at least two-thirds of us do not need jails and asylums and that we make the world better by our living in it. Any writer who confines himself to the third of us who are vicious or unfortunate and who fails to see the rest of us is telling us only a part of the truth. Perhaps the novelist is not wholly at fault for his poor vision; yet many others than Pilate have asked the question, "What is truth?" and have failed to wait for the answer.

It is not good for us human beings to concentrate our attention too much on the inhabitants of jails and asylums. We are so made that we need heroic exemplars to imitate. We need exalted motives, and exalted motives are frequently born of desire to imitate those we love and admire. Despite this human need our modern novelists furnish us, not examples to virtue but examples to vice. A reviewer in the New York *Evening Post* some years ago had this to say:

"We use the word animalism for the sake of clearness, to denote a species of realism which deals with man considered as an animal, capable of hunger, thirst, lust, cruelty, vanity, fear, sloth, predacity, greed, and other passions and appetites that make him kin to the brutes, but which neglects, as far as possible, any higher qualities which distinguish him from his four-footed relatives, such as humor, thought, reason, aspiration, affection, morality, and religion. Real life is full of the contrasts between these conflicting tendencies, but the object of the animalistic school seems always to make a study of the *genus homo* which shall recall the menagerie at feeding-time rather than human society."

If our so-called realists would be content to show us the menagerie merely at feeding time we should not find so much fault with them, but they show us the menagerie at pursuits much more dangerous and degrading than mere eating. This brings us to the moot question: What moral obligation has the writer? The moderns seem to have rejected all ideas of right and wrong. Taste is their criterion of judgment; expediency, their motive in action. All too many of them boast that they have no desire to remold the universe, that they have no "messianic passion." They have no desire to save the world from its evils; they wish only to draw pictures of its evils. Thus they prove their inferiority as men and as artists, one of the best definitions of art being "inspired utility." It takes no great skill on the part of a physician to recognize smallpox; it takes considerable skill to give the right medicine so as to effect a cure. The man who sees evil and tries to put good in its place, even though his idea of good be mistaken, is a greater man than the one who sees evil and says there is nothing to be done about it. There is evil all about us, and those who shut their eyes to it are fools, but they are the greater fools who see it and say that nothing can be done about it, and the greatest of all fools are those who say that there is nothing but evil round about us. These last are the so-called realists of to-day, who see nothing but asylums and jails amid a maze of buildings. Truly, as Shelley says, one of the first purposes of art is "to redeem from decay the visitations of the divinity in man"; and the surest way in which to accomplish this purpose is by preaching sanely and always unobtrusively the gospel of hope.

If we reject all ideas of right and wrong, we cannot of course talk about the moral obligations of the novelist. If taste be the final criterion of judgment, then the novelist may put all the filth and hopelessness he can find into his narrative, and no matter how much he jars our æsthetic feelings we shall not condemn him. But if, as every serious and right-thinking person knows without doubt, right and wrong are most important to the novelist, he has moral obligations that apply to himself in the act of writing and obligations that apply to his readers. There have been men of immoral lives who have produced great art, for the effect of immorality on the artist is, in many cases, negative; it keeps him from his highest achievement. The effect is almost always positive, that is, actually transmitted to his art when the art is literary. Writing is in many senses the man himself. Yet there have been men of evil lives who have produced literature with high moral value; perhaps because they have seen the beauty they are spoiling, so vividly as to be able to portray it vividly. But what shall we say of the artist whose personal life is praiseworthy and who yet writes literature of evil import?

This question introduces the morality of thought. There are comparatively few persons who can think on matters of sex with no effect on themselves. Most persons, on the other hand, can describe murder and theft and forgery and suicide or read descriptions of them with no awakened desire to imitate them. A novelist can in the course of his story make his characters commit any of these crimes and punish them accordingly without the slightest danger to himself or to his readers. There may be novelists who can think out sins against the sixth and ninth commandments so vividly as to be able to portray them and who yet get no personal reactions to their detailed thoughts, and there may be readers who can read their novels without dangerous reactions; but I think both novelists and readers of such kind are few. Even if the novelist is immune to sex temptations, he must remember that about ninety per cent of his readers are not immune; and if he brought temptation to even one reader, he would deserve censure. "One man's meat is another's poison" is a saying often incorrectly used.

An artist has, of course, the right to portray evil, for the simple reason that he is portraying life, and in life there is usually evil. He must not, however, make the evil attractive to his readers. Most readers have enough of temptations arising from themselves, their neighbors, and the devil to keep their wills strong and their consciences alert; they do not need the aid of the novelist. Familiarity with vice lessens the horror of it. When likable characters in fiction sin, the readers are moved to forgive not only the sinner but also the sin. The next and almost inevitable step is much easier forgiveness of self for the same or some similar sin. So long as sin in fiction is used for the purpose of purifying the reader through pity and fear, as Aristotle bade us use it in the drama, it is not likely to be dangerous, unless too picturesque in its presentation; so long as the lesson "the wages of sin is death" is taught, the author can as a rule save himself and his reader from the fascination which some sins possess in their very nature. It is very easy for the normal person to be tempted by sex sin, as most persons know by experience; and so the author who brings his reader, often unawares, into such temptation is doing him an irremediable harm.

In matters of faith the novelist has need to exercise the same care as in matters of purity. The scene in Hardy's *Tess of the D'Urberville's* in which the heroine is assaulted is not more dangerous than the author's query as to the whereabouts of God during this ugly crime, or the final dismissal of the whole sad story when Tess swings on the gallows, by the statement, " 'Justice' was done, and the President of the Immortals (in Æschylean phrase) had ended his sport with Tess." Hardy touches our faith on the raw as it were. There are times when the providence of God seems a bit unreal and when we cling blindly to faith as we walk through sorrow and shame. Writers of Hardy's ability can do just about as they please with their readers. They should not strike us in our weakest points.

A most pitiable quality of American literary criticism to-day is the fact that books are judged

only on artistic merit and not for their moral
values. Critics of the Mencken type who are
"unencumbered by dogma, free from the mania
of certitude" are doing us a vast amount of harm.
There is a dual standard in criticism. Plato
missed it because he judged all literature only by
the standard of its power to teach morality. Aristotle discovered it and taught that literature has
a twofold function, that is, to teach truth and to
give artistic or æsthetic pleasure. It is sad that
Bliss Perry and Hamilton Mabie and Stuart Sher-
man have to a great extent lost their prestige
among us, because they stood for fine traditions
which taught this twofold function of criticism.
They insisted that novelists tell the whole truth
and tell it artistically. They had no patience
with novelists who see only what is evil in life or
who are content to be mere photographers of the
externals of life or who distort life's beautiful
truths into vicious caricatures.

We all can see facts. It is the business of the
artist to get for us the truth behind facts. Only
the artist who knows truth is able to find it behind
facts. Only the artist who is fortified with certitude should dare to lay his hands on facts and
wrest their secrets from them.

V. THE FINE ARTS OF READING AND WRITING

ANY crimes are being committed to-day against the fine old arts of reading and writing. One of these crimes is of a commercial nature, having to do with the dime novel of dubious memory. Young people nowadays would not buy an old-fashioned dime novel; their novels must cost two dollars, even if their contents be worth less than those of the novels that used to sell for a dime, for it is in the case of the novel as in the case of everything else, it must cost several times its worth if it is to sell. Years ago, cheap books for cheap people were sold at their face value. Now, people whose souls are proportionately as cheap as their pockets are expensive want to buy cheap books for high prices. So the honest old dime novel has given way to the best seller.

Despite the régime of the best sellers, however, America is not a book-reading nation. In England the number of books published annually exceeds the numbers of magazines and newspapers. In America the opposite is true. *The*

Saturday Evening Post, The Ladies' Home Journal, and *The American Magazine* all boast over two million copies an issue, whereas any best seller among novels is happy to get into its second hundred thousand. Examine the magazine racks in a railroad station or let your eye travel along your Pullman, and you will know what the American public reads when it travels. Step into milord's office or milady's boudoir, and you will know what cultured Americans read during leisure hours.

The widespread addiction to these three magazines is in some ways hopeful as a testimony to the fundamental decency of the American reading public, for in them I have yet to meet a nasty story. But there are, on the other hand, a number of other magazines, almost equally popular, that are frankly salacious. As regards novels, conclusions as to our decency cannot be happy ones, for our novel writers and readers show a tendency to set aside moral values—surely a crime against one of the primary functions of the art of fiction. Even the old-fashioned dime novel, which most of us read surreptitiously and in a state of inward perturbation and shame, was comparatively clean beside many of the novels that are flaunted by their readers to-day. Then, too, these old novels made some pretense of pointing out the theme, "the wages of sin is death." They were, as a rule, silly rather than vicious: men got on their knees and recited amorous rhapsodies never heard in real life on land or sea, and girls mooned over dream-made lovers who would come riding on white chargers from some never-never land to carry them shrieking to a turreted castle. Oh, I grant that they were not true to life (after the wild, sweet fancies of young love have faded), but were they a thousandth part so in league with man's natural enemies to virtue as are the nasty sex novels and the morbidly pessimistic novels that have such vogue now?

Just as it did not avail to tell the young people of the past generation not to read the dime novel, so it does not avail to tell the young people of to-day not to read the salacious best sellers, because so long as these books are on the markets young people will read them. Despite the fact that our Catholic young people are surely warned sufficiently, they, too, seem to think little of the danger of indiscriminate reading. Forbidding them to read books is not enough; they must be given a substitute for the books forbidden. Waiving the books that are really harmful, the teacher is sometimes appalled by the poverty of contemporary fiction remaining. It does not help much to give the modern girl, in particular, the older novels; she wants modern fiction. She reads all the English poets from Chaucer to Browning with gracious ease and she thrills to Romeo or Cyrano at their poetic love-making; but she waves aside the old novels with a bored gesture and asks for the novels of to-day. Her brother, when he reads at all, is just as likely to take up Scott or Thackeray as Sinclair Lewis.

Our paramount need is good Catholic fiction, a need manifested by the frequency with which non-Catholic novelists adopt themes avowedly Catholic as well as by our own desire for it. We want, not the kind that obtrudes its religion, but the kind in which the characters live by their religion as good Catholics do in real life. If the heroine is a champion tennis player, the normal reader is far more interested in her tennis playing than in her religion. When, however, the Catholic tennis player chooses a husband, the novelist may insist properly that the reader come to a Church wedding or he may insist that the reader disapprove if the heroine run off to a justice of the peace. The heroine need not be aggressively Catholic when she enters upon her career as an opera singer after three years' apprenticeship as a public stenographer, but she must show herself not only as a Catholic but as an exceedingly thoughtful one when she abandons her artistic career to enter the Little Sisters of the Poor. The principal need of the Catholic novelist is, it seems to me, a sense of proportion. Because so many of our Catholic novelists lack this sense, we have much Catholic fiction that makes religion odious rather than attractive. God's grace works silently in our souls; and we should be content to let it work silently in the novels we write to help souls to appreciate God's grace.

There is an immense difference between the Catholic novelist and the Catholic who writes novels, but it is a difference that need not be always apparent. When the novelist deals only in externals his religion is not called into the work of creation in any direct fashion. So long as principles are not involved the Catholic novelist is not different from any other novelist. Since most of us are not called upon to make tremendous and therefore dramatic choices between right and wrong in our ordinary living, we naturally object to a hero or heroine who is forced to make such choices in at least every other chapter of his or her story. One or two choices are sufficient for the ordinary novel. Obviously, there may often be the necessity of a long preparation for the actual choice, but even in such cases there must not be endless analysis of character or the reader will be wearied. The principles at stake should be set forth briefly and intelligibly, but the reader should be spared from preachment. Though the ordinary reader submits more or less gracefully to his Sunday sermon, he does object to his novelist in the pulpit.

When questions of principle are at stake the Catholic novelist is bound to reason as a Catholic or as an anti-Catholic, for there is no middle ground here. A conspicuous example of a Catholic who treated ethical problems in a manner at variance with Catholic principles is Joseph Conrad. Man is in his novels frequently the victim of circumstances. Though it is true that the will of man is Conrad's hero, he is a hero unaided by God. Chateaubriand had the mind but not the heart of the Catholic. Balzac's novels give us characters who live in a Christian atmosphere but are governed by naturalistic principles. These three are novelists of great power, who might have written tremendous Catholic fiction. They are but three among several Catholics of genuine ability who have failed to tell us the truth for which we ask. In America our Catholic novelists seem not so much to have written fiction that is anti-Catholic as to have written fiction that is wholly secular in character.

American Catholics have been true to themselves in poetry and philosophy, but they have turned over their beautiful fictional subjects to outsiders. For example, they left the epic of the religious vocation to Fannie Hurst, who surely could not understand it so well as they do, and she sold it to thousands under the title, *Appassionata*. Our Catholic novelist may retort with truth, if a Catholic novelist had written *Appassionata* the book would never have found a publisher. For some strange reason, perhaps because of Catholic indifference, avowedly Catholic fiction does not find an appreciable market in America. The giant Dostoevski swayed all Europe with his tremendous Catholic dogma, *"Fiat voluntas Tua,"* a doctrine which blooms like a tall white lily amid the dark, dreadful marshes of his scenes. Monsignor Benson immortalized for English-speaking people the whole of Catholic Church history under the Tudors in such fashion as to warrant continuous reprinting of his novels. Enid Dennis blithely invents a riot of miracles, which are swallowed without a grimace by an encouraging number of people even in America. The fault of a poor market for Catholic fiction in the United States lies, it seems to me, not at the door of the reading public but at the door of the novelists whose fiction is not vital and interesting enough to win favor.

Catholicism is the heart of every great artistic achievement, for the simple reasons that truth is the subject matter of great art and Catholicism is truth. Great art is the one earthly immortality, the one way in which the soul may live on earth after death. Long ago Plato told us, "Books are the immortal sons defying their sires." St. Thomas, who built his philosophy of the beautiful on the teachings of Aristotle, tells us that the reason for the continuance of great art is its power to give mental pleasure, no matter how often the mind comes back to it.

Books that live have in them this power to give pleasure to the mind. In every great book, no matter how purely emotional it may seem to be, is that something in which the mind rests. This rest of the mind is not a simple inertia or sleep; it is rather an active feeding of the mind, exemplified in poor fashion by the sleep during which the body rebuilds its energy. Just as great books feed the mind on good food, so do evil books give the mind small doses of poison. Though the human body can get rid of small doses of poison the mind cannot do so, for it has a fatal power of storing everything that enters it in the subconscious.

In an issue of *The Bookman* I read of an old man who said that he never reads anything except the Sears, Roebuck Catalogue because he considers reading a waste of time. Life, according to him, is too full to allow time for reading. Though it is true that the development of the mind is aided by study of other people, though it is true that we become cultured by association with cultured people, it is rather stupid to think that such association should be confined to those immediately about us. Culture may be secured by association with the great ones of the past, and the only means to such association is books. In books we find the intimate stories of some of the greatest people who have graced earth by living on it, for example, the saints of God. Shutting oneself off from the cares and distractions of daily living, in the company of the saints, is without doubt the highest kind of cultural pursuit. I cannot think of a better training school for the gentleman than a few hours spent daily in the company of St. Francis de Sales. This saint lived in interesting times. Why does not some Catholic of literary genius weave about him a living, breathing romance? About the glorious St. Bernard a tremendous historical novel could be woven, with all the glamor of the Crusades for its background. Cooper immortalized the American forest for us, but Blessed Isaac Jogues turned that forest into a vestibule of Paradise. And yet our Catholics in America spin insipid yarns of boarding school misses and soda clerks, while these divine romances lie unwritten. We are content to write dime novels in two-dollar jackets when we might write those that are purchased in coin of Heaven. Biographies of saints sell satisfactorily, even when written as miserably as some of them are; and there is no reason to believe that novels written around them would not sell—if cash and not art is to be the motive that spurs our novelist to write.

Ruskin's beautiful tribute to the good woman may be applied also to the good book: "The path of a good woman is indeed strewn with flowers; but they rise behind her steps, not before them." The good book leaves in its wake flowers of courage, idealism, kindliness. To write a good book one must discover the best that is in oneself. Getting acquainted with oneself ought to make for culture as well as for spiritual growth, and yet it is a kind of cultural process that is too little understood in these distracted days. Thinking in one's heart is the best preparation for writing; and the dearth of good writing shows that the land is indeed made desolate for want of thinking in the heart.

Booksellers may tell us that writers dare not be thoughtful because their readers do not want to be made to think. This is not true. People do not want to do laborious thinking; they want their thoughts wrapped in the mazes of charming narrative and laughter. Just as people want all the conveniences of physical life so they want conveniences in their mental life. An illustration of this fact is the sale of Will Durant's *Story of Philosophy* and George Dorsey's *Why We Behave Like Human Beings,* which are read by thousands of earnest but blind seekers for the Way, the Truth, and the Life, who are grasping at any helping hand, even though it lead them into the pit. To use narrative as a vehicle for truth is no new procedure to us Catholics; the Founder of our Church taught us that stories are an excellent means of teaching truth.

To write a book of high spiritual and mental quality is in itself an education. If the book be of critical or biographical character one must go through a long, severe course of intensive reading which will fill the mind with well-organized matter and then one must make this matter a very part of oneself. One must discuss the subject with others and thus make it clear in one's own mind and amenable to expression to others. Thus one educates oneself in the true meaning of the term, to draw forth from.

All this reads like a special plea. It is. I wish every one who likes good novels would enter into a crusade to force our Catholic novelists to write great Catholic novels, Catholic in every sense and great according to the novelist's limitations. We have a right to be indignant with those writers of genius who avoid Catholic subjects or who handle them in an antagonistic spirit. We have an equal right to be indignant with those who should not write at all but who insist on writing what they think is Catholic fiction. Would that their friends were more discriminating than kind!

VI. A PLEA FOR SALUTARY SENTIMENTALISM

OUR age is the heyday of cynical sophistication. When a writer dares to put into a book a bit of old-fashioned sentiment, the critics straightway take up pens, which are meant to be pointed but which are warped instead, and write the puffy word "Piffle," and the youthful readers languidly murmur their oozy damning "Slush." Yet the one thing above all that we need to-day is a little saving sentimentalism. One would, of course, hesitate to recommend in its entirety the sentimentalism of Richardson's time, which I beg leave to describe again. The entire family were assembled on long winter evenings to hear the father read aloud some interminable novel, and, during the reading, when certain harrowing passages of that novel were finished, were permitted to retire to separate rooms to weep. At any rate, one must at least note the fact that the entire family were assembled for the evenings, and must repeat that it would be difficult to imagine such an assembly in the modern home, which is now considered such a desirable place to get away from every evening.

There are two current views regarding the emotions, neither of which is worthy of the Christian. There is the rigorist view, which regards the emotions and passions as bad in themselves and therefore forbids under pain of sin the slightest indulgence of them. Opposed to this view is that of the immoralists, who teach that the passions are in themselves good and that the unrestrained indulgence of them is the highest activity of man. It is easy to see how the inevitable revolt against the first view aided by the sanction of the second has brought about the disastrous licenses of our young people to-day. The Christian teaching holds the happy mean: the emotions and passions are in themselves neither morally good nor evil but indifferent, and indifferently capable of great evil or great good. They are a powerful motor force in human conduct, to be directed to the service of God and the development of men.

The cynic, who differs from the evolutionist in thinking that man is getting worse instead of better as ages roll along, has perhaps some justification for his languid gesture toward modern humanity and his utterly weary comment, "See for yourself how hopeless things are." Whether

he be rigorist or Christian his reaction is the same.
One of his appalling tendencies is to sneer at the
emotional as ridiculous, or, and this is even worse,
to leer at the emotional as licentious.

From the metaphysical point of view the passions and emotions, being creatures of God, are
good. They are so essential to human nature and
conduct that we cannot tolerate even in fiction
a character who lacks any of them notably. Great
literature is always full of sentiment, for the simple reason that great literature is above all things
human. One of the masterpieces of tragic literature is "Macbeth." It may be straining the quotation a trifle to explain as a complaint against
Macbeth's sentimentalism Lady Macbeth's observation that her husband was "too full of the
milk of human kindness" to murder his cousin the
king. Indeed, the lady herself lapsed into what
the moderns would term sorry sentimentalism
when she refrained from driving the dagger into
the heart of the sleeping king, for the absurdly
human reason that he resembled her father. One
can easily imagine the fate that the critic of the
Mencken type would award to the contemporary
dramatist who would dare to put such a human
touch into a play. No, the modern heroine must
sneer at the fancied resemblance and at its effect

on her as being a sign of weakness, if the obstacle
in her path happens to be an old king; or, in the
way of Ibsen's Nora, she must walk sternly out
the door to her "freedom," if the obstacle happens to be two or three sleeping children. Lady
Macbeth may have been sentimental in not killing
the old king with her own hand; and yet this act
and the motherly quality of her love for Macbeth when he showed weakness at the sight of
Banquo's ghost make her something more of a
woman and something less of the sexless monster.

Women are, as a rule, more sentimental than
men. Who is more sentimental than the right
kind of mother? Who else would ever sit down
to cry over the scuffed baby shoe of a grown-up
boy who has just told her that another woman
has come into his life? Even the most scornful
cynic must doff his hat to that picture. Unashamed sentiment belongs to age rather than to
youth; it finds most perfect expression in those
for whom the passionate demands of young
healthy love have faded into peaceful and hazy
memories. It could scarcely come unblemished
to those who have lived licentious lives, because
their emotional life is stunted and decayed by
their very excesses. Just as one naturally expects
more rebellion in the passions and more ruthless

cruelty in the judgment of the young, so one should naturally expect well-disciplined passions and more of the "milk of human kindness" in the old. What is this milk of human kindness if it be not kinship of sentiment? The more genuinely human one is, the more is one sentimental. Not without reason do we call a cruel woman unwomanly and therefore unnatural. We should have found Lady Macbeth altogether impossible without her slightly redeeming manifestations of sentiment, which the cynic may call weakness but which in reality were her strength.

Women have not, however, a monopoly on sentiment; they simply dare to express their emotions in word and in act, whereas men are by conventional forces restrained in emotional expression of the more tender kind. In so far as conventions are concerned, one is almost constrained to admit that they were kinder to men in more barbarous times than in the days of chivalry. In those rude old days to secure a wife was not so harrowing to a man's sensibilities. All the cave man needed to do was to sight an attractive damsel, hit her over the head with a club, and lug her home to be his own particular servant thereafter. Chivalry ruined this nicely ordered scheme of things. It forced a man to balance perilously on one knee whilst he tried to twist his stiff and unwilling tongue about certain poetic phrases, used never before and certainly never to be used again. And in many cases there must have been a feminine impulse, strangled only by the fear that he might depart peaceably though irrevocably, to refuse the man in order to induce him to resort to the methods of more primitive times when men, not women, governed the procedure of courtship. We hear much talk nowadays about reversion to the "cave man" style. "Away with chivalry" cries the feminine Don Quixote. If she keeps on drinking and smoking and wearing scant dresses, away will go poor old chivalry, sighing for his dear youth when women dwelt on pedestals and men knelt before them. The while he clings to the few lingering garments of his glory, the frank, comradely equality of our boys and girls is to be admired, even if proposals of marriage must be shouted to the whistling wind above the roar of an engine hitting its fifty miles an hour.

The term sentimentality has been so linked to the love of courtship that its broader meaning has been obscured. There are many emotions besides love, and many loves besides the love of man and woman that culminates in marriage.

Many of life's most beautiful sentiments are in no way connected with such love. Many of the most beautiful dramas and novels have no such love in them, and yet are filled with deep and tender sentiment. "Ah, yes," murmurs the cynical critic, who is so occupied in splitting hairs as to lose the effect of the whole Marcel, "but you confuse sentimentality with sentiment." In self-defense one must say that Webster, who surely splits hairs with noble art, makes no distinction between the two terms, except to note that the term sentimentality is often used to mean excessive sentimental manifestation. Now, if sentimental and sentimentalism and sentimentality are not the adjective and the nouns that name aright manifestations of sentiment, some one will have to come to the assistance of Mr. Webster by coining new words. While we await this clever person let us use the adjective and nouns as defined by the dictionary, to mean normal manifestation of sentiment. We do not condemn ice cream because some people eat it excessively, nor do we condemn sentimentality because Sterne wept over a donkey which had to work rather than eat macaroons. If Sterne had shed those tears over a child in the sweatshop industry, he would have showed himself less the donkey and more the man. In this mistake of his is the exact difference between him and Dickens. One of the few hopeful things in modern fictional output is the fact that the novels of Dickens continue to be among the world's best sellers, and that there still are those to pay them the tribute of tears. Yet all too many critics call him maudlin.

Love, the most beautiful of all sentiments, is the motive power of life, and therefore of much literature. Love of parents, of children, of home, of country, of honor, and, above all, the love of God, are loves that have been the themes of great literature. The most sentimental and at the same time the most beautiful story ever told is the story of the Master's life and love. The only Perfect One who has graced the earth by living on it was as perfect in His sentiments as in every other respect. Even in the aspect of sentimentalism most sneered at to-day, that is, the public display of emotion, our Lord showed Himself sentimental. Consider, for example, the death of Lazarus. The Master went with Mary and Martha to the tomb of their brother and, seeing their great sorrow, He wept. One must wonder at His grief. He knew that in a moment He would turn their sorrow to intense joy by the miracle of raising Lazarus to life; and yet, with the sympathy of the tenderest Heart that ever beat in human breast He knew their woe of the last four days. He had hurt them by His failure to come in their need. There is no anguish more poignant than that resulting from the knowledge of having hurt those one loves. Jesus felt this anguish so keenly that He wept. Then, He too, in turn, must have been hurt by their apparent want of trust in Him. Like all human beings, our Lord doubtless wanted His loved ones to keep on believing in Him even after He had given them what seemed good reason to disbelieve in Him. It would be interesting to hear the comments that the modern critic would make concerning this incident if he should treat it as he treats fiction which dares to contain some normal human sentiment.

This is only one example of the sentimentalism of our Lord. He is God as well as man; and His humanity is perfect because it is fashioned to the image and likeness of God. We do not emphasize sufficiently the fact that human nature is modeled on the divine and that therefore the more one is human, the more one is like God. Our Lord, as we know when we look at a Crucifix, was strong and stern. No weakling could thus have held pain to His heart and at the same time have looked levelly into the leering eyes of shame. Jesus was every inch the ideal man, and yet so boyishly in love was He with the face and voice of a certain sweet Lady that He seemed to upset all His divine plans, to change some water into wine, simply because she did not want a bride and groom to suffer an embarrassment on their wedding day. Our cynic would make short work of this.

The saints understand the truth that humanity is Godlike, and they are most human, despite the efforts of many well-meaning biographers to make them over into Puritans. Saints know that all human qualities are good, and that the lack of human qualities is evil. Saints never try to kill their emotions; they simply use them rightly to their fullest extent. Saints do things so sentimental that the rigorist must needs condemn their acts as illegitimate and the cynic must sneer at them as just plain maudlin. There was that silly Francis of Assisi, for example, who once got down from his horse to kiss a leper on the mouth, so that the poor creature might for a moment feel human again. There was that ridiculous Francis Xavier who took the discipline for the sins of his friend the merchant so that the easy-going fellow might not have to hurt his own tender skin. There was that soft-hearted Scholastica who wanted a few more hours with her brother Benedict and cried so hard to get them that God sent a storm just to quiet her and keep Benedict with her for the night. There was, finally, that foolish Little Flower with her everlasting use of the word "love" in her autobiography and her abandoned infatuation with Jesus, which sapped all her physical strength and killed her when she was only twenty-four years old—killed her, it seems, only that she might come back to live on earth in a lovelier way! Truly, these saints are shockingly sentimental. Yet, if these be sentimentalists, let us have more of them.

What we need to-day is a return to sentiment— good, clean, wholesome sentiment. Even our children are learning to sneer at honest affection. The cinema spreads before the wondering eyes of the ten-year-old exaggerated expressions of passion, which at first bewilder and then demoralize as the meaning of the pictures dawns in the curious mind. Little girls who ought to be playing with dolls paint their faces and smirk at every man they meet, and their astounded parents forget the picture shows and the salacious magazines, for the existence of which they are responsible, and lament the times in which they must live. If we could but get our children nowadays to read

the literature that has home and love and honor
in it, if we could but get home and love and honor
on the screen, the next generation would not be
so pleasure-mad and utterly reckless as is this
one. Our literature is getting far from the once-
deserved characterization of Chesterton:

"I know few men in England who have not left
their boyhood to some extent lost and entangled
in the forests of *Huckleberry Finn*. I know few
women . . . who will not confess to having
passed a happy childhood with the *Little Women*
of Miss Alcott. *Helen's Babies* was the first and
by far the best book in the modern scriptures
of baby-worship. And about all this old-fashioned
American literature there was an indefinable savour that satisfied and even pleased our growing
minds. Perhaps it was the smell of growing
things, but I am far from certain that it was not
simply the smell of wood."

Happy indeed were the pioneers whose pleasures were so few and whose interests were so limited that they had time to think and write and
read about such simple things as home and love
and honor. Happy indeed were they because they
were not ashamed to be sentimental.

Could we be Christians in our mental and emotional lives, we should be much more normal and

much more joyful. We should dare to take life's legitimate pleasures and use them happily, or, if God so pleased, we should, understanding and loving them, lay them on the high altar of sacrifice for His honor and our own sanctification. We should dare to write healthy human literature instead of the "erotic, neurotic, Tommyrotic" stuff now being produced so abundantly. We should even dare to be openly and unashamedly in love with God and humanity and nature. We should, if God gave us strength, in the manner of Francis of Assisi, sing canticles to our brother the sun and yet welcome the painful blindness that brings darkness to be offered in penance for the sins of others. We should, in a word, cheerfully gird ourselves and go out to do battle on the highroad to Paradise, clad in the white armor of truth, bearing the shield of charity, and wielding the lance of justice.

VII. THE BIBLE AS A MEANS TO LITERARY TRAINING

HEN Thomas à Kempis said, among many other salutary remarks, that "truth is to be sought for in Holy scriptures, not eloquence," he, being wise as well as good, did not thereby put his veto upon the use of the Bible as a school for literary training. Being mindful that spiritual profit is to be sought first, we can nowhere in a single source find so much to help us in literary ways. It is part of our discipline as Catholics to understand that we need an infallible interpreter of the Bible, because it is difficult in parts and is therefore in many places subject to erroneous interpretations. We are not concerned here with the Bible as a training school for virtues, among them docile faith, and yet there is one virtue which is so inextricably molded into the fiber of the good writer that it commands attention. This is the virtue of humility, without which one can never develop one's full powers. Lack of humility causes either fatal overconfidence in one's own powers or, which is perhaps worse, lack of confidence in them.

Humility is enjoined on us as an obligation. "Learn of me," said the Master, "because I am meek and humble of heart." Is it not of worth in our estimate of intellectual and literary values to study the teaching methods of Wisdom Himself, for is not every good writer a teacher of truth? Any child can understand the lessons of the Master, for He couched His teachings in the language of the ordinary person. And yet it is language which could be improved by no artifice of style. It was the priests and the doctors of the law who found difficulty in understanding Christ, never the common folk who came to Him. Pride and deceitfulness can never understand humility and truth.

Simplicity, the simplicity that is power, is the fundamental characteristic of the Scriptures. From the simple statement, with all its connotative power, "In the beginning God created heaven and earth," to the blessing which wishes all blessedness, "the grace of our Lord Jesus Christ be with you all," the Book of books is throughout strong and stirring by its expressive simplicity. Economy of words is the handmaid to simplicity, and truly she walks in Biblical phrasing. In George Lewes' treatise *Principles of Success in*

Literature, is this interesting comment on economy in style.

" 'God said: Let there be light: and there was light.' This is a conception of power so calm and simple that it needs only to be presented in the fewest and the plainest words, and would be confused or weakened by any suggestion of accessories. Let us amplify the expression in the redundant style of miscalled eloquent writers: 'God, in the magnificent fulness of creative energy, exclaimed: Let there be light! and lo! the agitating fiat immediately went forth and thus in one indivisible moment the whole universe was illumined!' We have here a sentence which I am certain many a writer would, in secret, prefer to the masterly plainness of Genesis. It is not a sentence which would have captivated critics."

One could multiply illustrations after the example of Mr. Lewes, but he makes the point with sufficient effectiveness. The Gospels are conspicuous for their want of unnecessary details in their record of Christ's life on earth. Reticence is the surest indication of delicacy in matters intimate and spiritual, and, were it nothing more, the reticence of the Gospel narrators concerning the first visit of the Risen Christ to His Mother and to St. Peter would still be the highest kind of artistic achievement. So, too, the exquisite artistry of the narrators is evidenced in their treatment of the Passion of Christ, which stirs in its readers an anguish that is too deep for the relief of tears. Deftly, exquisitely, the pictures are drawn, to remain ineradicably traced on the reader's heart. "And the Lord turning, looked on Peter. And Peter, going out, wept bitterly." "And there stood by the cross of Jesus, His Mother."

One of the particular beauties of the Bible is the rhythmic flow of its language, a charm which is the despair of all imitators. The prayer that is song breathes through every page of the Psalms. "O God, my God, to Thee do I watch at the break of day. For Thee my soul hath thirsted; for Thee my flesh, O how many ways!" In trying to explain to my students what is meant by prose rhythm I often ask them to read aloud in turn certain portions of the Psalms, the Prophecies, or the Gospels. Invariably, after reading a few verses, they begin to let their voices rise and fall in a rhythm that is peculiarly Biblical. Then I call their attention to the effect which they are unconsciously producing. After the first experiment of this kind in the early part of the scholastic year, the next set of compositions usually evidence a marked effort to secure rhythm. Sometimes the efforts are in a measure successful, and sometimes they result in effects which are ludicrous. The efforts are of consequence, however, for they show that the sense for the beautiful has been stimulated. From the fact that such a large number of artists in prose attribute their success to assiduous reading of the Bible, I believe it is no exaggeration to conclude that the Bible is the finest literary training school there is; and I am convinced that any one who reads the Bible for a half hour a day with a seeing eye and an understanding ear will soon acquire mastery of the sound values of words and the harmonies of phrasing.

The peculiar Biblical rhythm is produced by a parallelism of structure, a balancing of line with line and of phrase with phrase. Sonorousness of sound and sublimity of idea are confined within simple, searching, eloquent poetry. This haunting rhythm is especially evident in the Book of Job, and it is very beautiful in Eliu's discourse on the power and wisdom of God. "Who teacheth us more than the beasts of the earth, and instructeth us more than the fowls of the air?" asks the son of Barachel in his anger at Job, only to be answered by the Lord out of a whirlwind: "Who is this that wrappeth up sentences in unskillful words? . . . Hast thou entered into the depths of the sea, and walked in the lowest parts of the deep? Have the gates of death been opened to thee, and hast thou seen the darksome doors?" Very often the rhetorical question, such an integral part of the Biblical style, is given its answer as a means to further the parallelism. "The Lord said to Job: Shall he that contendeth with God be so easily silenced? Surely he that reproveth God, ought to answer Him." And Job made reply: "What can I answer, who hath spoken inconsiderately? I will lay my hands upon my mouth." Nobly beautiful is this Book of Job, a book for all men. "It is our first, oldest statement," says Carlyle, "of the never-ending Problem—man's destiny, and God's ways with him here in this earth. And all in such free flowing outlines: grand in its sincerity, in its simplicity, in its epic melody, and repose of reconcilement."

The Book of Job is a great epic which touches the heights and depths of human experience. There are the manner of the Platonic dialogue in the controversies of Job with his friends and the method of Sophocles in the tragedy piled upon tragedy to a dramatic climax. Here one may well ask, Is there any literary form which does not consciously or unconsciously plagiarize the Bible?

Books might be written on the literary forms

of the Bible. There are the aphoristic glories of Proverbs and Ecclesiastes, the impassioned eloquence of the Prophecies, the perfect short stories of Joseph, Ruth, Tobias, Esther, and Judith, the poetry of the Psalms, the parables of the Gospels, the graphic history of the Acts of the Apostles, the Epistles, the imagery and the drama of the Apocalypse, all of which have vital significance for those who teach or write literature. Art is well defined as "inspired utility"; and this definition is especially applicable to the literary art of the Bible, wherein every sentence is the inspired expression of a salutary truth. One may open the Gospels at random and gather from any page the pearls of wisdom that the Master casts before us.

"I have called you friends: because all things whatsoever I have heard of My Father, I have made known to you." Here is truth. "Come unto Me." Here is love. "Amen I say to you, unless you be converted, and become as little children, you shall not enter into the kingdom of Heaven." Here is the lesson in humility. "Amen, amen, I say to you: if you ask the Father anything in My name, he will give it to you." Here is the ground of hope. "Let not your heart be troubled, nor let it be afraid." Here is assurance of peace.

"Greater love than this no man hath, that a man lay down his life for his friends." Here is the word of truth, the spirit that can bring forth life from death.

I can conceive no more perfect artistry than such language, with the whole foundation of a tremendous virtue caught in one small phrase, as if Vulcan took to working in filigree. Artistry in words was to be expected from Him who sees that each rose leaf is in place. One day when I was teaching some ponderous literature to a class and felt that their attention was due to a genuine effort, I was interrupted by a sparrow which perched on the window sill and, with an unmistakable question in his chirp, demanded again and again to know just what stupid thing all we motionless creatures were doing. Involuntarily the girls' eyes turned from my face to seek the saucy fellow with his perky head and flirting tail; involuntarily and even unconsciously, I think, tender little smiles appeared on the girls' lips. Not being in the least a pedagogical sort of person, I stopped talking about literature long since made and started to make some then and there, by the simple process of asking the question, "What does he make you think of?" "God made Him birds in a pleasant humour," quoted one girl. "Are not five sparrows sold for two farthings, and not one of them is forgotten before God?" quoted another, "Fear not, therefore: you are of more value than many sparrows." I hope that not even one girl in that class will fail to remember the Biblical quotation when sorrow comes to her in after years, even though every girl forgets the book we were discussing when the first friendly little chirp sounded from the window sill.

Literature is made of the very stuff of life, and the more our lives are molded and directed by the Bible the more capable we shall be of producing great literature. To write greatly is almost impossible to one who does not live greatly. Milton told us that the life of a great poet should be in itself a great poem. One of the surest means to great living is the daily reading of the Gospel, for thus we keep before our minds the example of Christ. There can, then, be no doubt that the finest training school for the writer is the Bible, which gives him both the matter and the manner of his art.

VIII. THE PIONEER IN PAGEANTRY AT WORK

HE drama was born at the altar, but it has wandered far indeed from its birthplace. Again and again it has come home like the prodigal, to be clothed once more in its pristine splendor; again and again it has heard the luring call of secularism and has been led away only to be despoiled. From the twelfth to the sixteenth century the English drama was, as it should be, the handmaid of religion; on the English stage of the twelfth and thirteenth centuries was presented by the people themselves the Miracle or Mystery Play, which furnished a historical presentation of Biblical scenes; during the two following centuries flourished the Morality Play, which personified vices and virtues in their everlasting conflict over the central figure, Man. In the sixteenth century the drama abandoned the religious themes and became secular in character, as it still is. For a time it kept to the high plane established by Shakespeare; then, in the Restoration Period, it became thoroughly immoral. Reformed, but never again wholly devoted to the service of religion, the drama has been kept fairly respectable, until in our day, being again degraded, it has exceeded the excesses of the Restoration. To counteract this tendency to evil the Little Theater movement has been organized. Another movement closely related to this one is the revival of the pageant and the masque, forms antecedent to the drama and of such possibilities as to employ a whole community in their presentation.

The pioneer in the movement to restore pageantry is the Reverend Daniel A. Lord, S.J., who has produced pageants that are genuine community endeavors in a dozen or more of the largest cities of the United States. The mere fact that there are anywhere from two to six hundred active participants in every pageant, not including the interested relatives and friends of the actors, shows the magnitude of the pageant's possibilities. In no case is a professional actor allowed to take part in one of these pageants, though somehow or other Father Lord always manages to secure the largest theater and the finest orchestra and the most skilled electricians and the cleverest costume designers of the city to contribute services, perhaps through his own persuasive powers, perhaps because the persons in question are naturally interested in such an ideal expression of community artistic endeavor. The audience, that most indispensable means to success, never fails in its duty, and it has yet to make any pageant a financial failure; in fact, it has shown a disposition to pay smilingly for standing room.

During Father Lord's years as student and teacher at St. Louis University after his graduation from Loyola in Chicago he wrote and produced three plays, and through this work learned how to be a successful director of amateur actors. His first pageant, "Alma Mater," was produced in 1920 by the students of St. Louis University, the alumni, society people, and associated schools. The first mission pageant, "The Dreamer Awakes," was produced in St. Louis in 1922 by the students of all the Catholic schools of this city, and it has been produced since that time in Washington, Pittsburgh, Brooklyn, Cincinnati, and other cities, with such success that about 150,000 persons have seen it. The next pageant, "The Pageant of Youth," was produced as a community affair in St. Mary's, Kansas, in Chicago in 1923, where is was played to immense audiences every night for a week, in Denver, Kansas City, Scranton, Columbus, San Francisco, and elsewhere. In 1924, "The Pageant of Peace" was produced in Chicago by the schools and ran for ten nights. Father Lord's latest pageant, "The Giant-Killer," ran at the Odeon Theater in St. Louis during Thanksgiving week of 1926 and was played to "standing room only." This synopsis gives of course no idea of the greatness of each undertaking, but in terms of cash, which are easily understood, it means that audiences in these cities were willing to pay the cost of production ranging from eight to fifteen thousand dollars and also furnish a very respectable sum over and above for charity to the missions. Father Lord's great success with the pageant and the one-act play makes one wish he would try his hand at regular drama.

Father Lord's pageants are allegorical in their foundation idea, but there is sufficient drama in them to save them from the obvious preaching even of the Morality Play. A brief analysis of "The Giant-Killer" will make this matter of composition clear. The author built his pageant on the tale of Jack-the-Giant-Killer.

"Once upon a time, as we read in all good fairy stories, a terrible giant walked with seven-league boots the highways and villages of Europe. His thunderous heels crushed through cottage roofs; his war club circled and struck with the force of a falling pine; he breakfasted off tender children, lunched off delicate maidens, dined off stalwart men. No wonder, then, that the countryside feared him and sent a yearly tribute of men and maidens to keep his yawning larder stocked. For, if the tribute failed, the crunch of his boots was heard over the roadways, and whole villages fell in ruins as he rushed on to his vengeance. 'Fee, fi, fo, fum!' bellowed his terrible voice; and strong men quaked, and children crouched in dark places, and women prayed piteously for a deliverer.

"Then came a brave and merry youth, Jack, by name. Alone, fearlessly, he sallied forth, met the giant in his lair, slew him with his own strong young hands, set free the prisoners in the giant's cave, and marched down through history the best beloved of our nursery heroes, Jack-the-Giant-Killer.

"This is the story of what happened 'once upon a time!' But every generation has its giants, and every generation cries aloud for its Jack.

"Over whole countries, casting a black shadow that blights villages and stunts human lives, broods to-day a sinister and ugly giant. He crushes men's bodies with grinding toil and holds men's minds in slavery. Little children are slain because it pleases him to see them die; women weep in chains of shameful slavery; men groan under his tyranny and look forward willingly to death that will open an escape from his power. He is the giant that rules two-thirds of the modern world, the giant whose servants are superstition and ignorance; he is Paganism.

"But into the world has come another Jack. He is marching with brave heart and courageous hand to slay this monster who preys on women, sacrifices children, and enslaves men. He has vowed that this giant shall fall before him as that other giant fell before another Jack. For he is the new Giant-Killer. He is the new Crusader fighting evil. He is Jack of the Catholic Students' Mission Crusade."

There is the allegory. The two parts of it were made into episodes. The olden day drama was presented in five separate scenes: a village fair in a medieval village, the cave of the giant, the road to the giant's cave, outside the giant's cave, inside the giant's cave. The modern day drama was presented in four scenes: the cave of Paganism, the courtyard of the castle of St. Louis the King, the cave of Paganism, the village square. By the plan of having the pageant played "all over the house," intermissions were eliminated between several pairs of scenes. In Part I, Scene 4, for example, the actors were all in the aisles of the theater or on the very front of the stage. The dramatic effect was thrilling: Jack found his way down the center aisle while will-o'-the-wisps in rainbow dresses and floating streamers opposed his progress in fantastic dance; ghosts slithered up and down the side aisles; witches glided in weird dance across the black background of the stage front; while over them all, strange, unearthly lights glowed, and vibrant music snarled and hissed and whispered and cried.

Father Lord tells his story three times: first in music, furnished by the finest symphony orchestra he can secure; second in dances, which are interpretative in character; third in action. The actors speak, of course, but only when speech is natural and incidental to the action. The essence of all drama is action, and there is never a lack of action in good pageantry; in fact, if there is any fault at all to be found in pageantry of Father Lord's making, it is that there is too much to watch, surely the happiest of faults, for it makes one wish to see the same show several times.

The wonder arises when one sees several hundred actors on a stage all doing something and doing it excellently, how did one man train them all? This brings us to the actual presentation of the pageant. Characters and dance groups are apportioned out by the director among schools; dramatic and athletic instructors coach the various groups; then the trained groups are brought together in a harmoniously related whole in a few general rehearsals under the general director. In a production of "The Giant-Killer" all the rehearsals were held after school hours and on holidays. The interest in them was manifested by a one hundred per cent attendance. Five weeks was the time allowed for the preparation of the pageant. On the day before the first show a dress rehearsal was given, with orchestra and lighting effects.

I had the privilege of attending both the dress rehearsal and the first performance of "The Giant-Killer," and I carried away with me the conviction that the pageant is one of the finest forces for good in the world. When I walked into the Odeon Theater in St. Louis at ten o'clock on the Friday morning after Thanksgiving Day, rehearsal had been in full swing for two hours. I saw first a stage filled with boys and girls of all ages, then fifty interested musicians in the orchestra chairs, then dozens and dozens of boys and girls sitting in the pit of the theater, silent, and with their eyes on the stage. My first thought was that the boys and girls in the audience had been invited to the dress rehearsal. Then I heard a sharp command: "Clear the stage." In an incredibly short time and in silence, the stage was cleared and those coming from it were seated in groups in the pit of the theater. Then came a second command: "Second episode on stage." My erstwhile audience stirred. About two hundred of them were on the stage before I realized what they were doing. I settled myself to see the show, but again I heard: "Clear the stage." Then I perceived that this was just a rehearsal for orchestra cues. After I learned that there were exactly forty-five cues, I understood the need for rehearsal. The orchestra, under the direction of Mr. Noël Poepping, furnished a musical setting for the pageant that was a real artistic triumph. If the audience got nothing else but that orchestra's rendition of Father Lord's exquisitely composed program of music, it would get a most lovely evening of art.

Though the rehearsal was a distinct disappointment so far as seeing the show was concerned and left me in a sort of frenzy of impatience for the first performance, it gave me an intimate knowledge of the mechanism of pageantry. There were a few hitches, of course, or the rehearsal would not have run true to life. Some of them were unutterably funny. There were, for example, about fifty little girls who had waited patiently—that is, to some degree—for their turn to get on the stage and do their dance. When at last the longed-for command came: "Pigmies and victims on stage," there was a happy bustle and a liberal assortment of smiles. With unbelievable swiftness each tiny lady was in her place, poised for her dance. Suddenly the smiles were blotted from the little faces by the stern command: "Clear the stage." Their keening Irish ancestors or wailing Jewish ones would have been proud of the lamentations that filled the air: woe unutterable shook the little figures as they trailed rebelliously to their places, and after the manner of children each child thought any available portion of the director's person was the one requisite spot to soak up her tears. Even this consolation was denied them; the show had to go on, because the orchestra was being paid for by the hour.

The little folks in the pageant are of course the loveliest part of it, though, in the way of little folks, they meet with tragedies innumerable and create all sorts of embarrassing difficulties for the director. There was the small girl, for example, who just before her scene came sobbing frantically across the stage with one nicely stockinged leg and one bare foot to demand that another stocking be handed out immediately to take the place of the lost one. Stage hands, orchestra, 449 other actors, audience—everything had to be forgotten till that stocking was secured; for who could let a child miss her part in the first performance of her first show?

Naturally I expected something like a riot behind the scenes when I contemplated 450 boys and girls of all ages in such close quarters. On the contrary, the order was perfect. The groups in each episode appeared at a stated time, and left the theater immediately after their episode had been played, thus making way for the next groups. The dressing rooms were assigned according to schools, and older boys and girls appointed to take care of the younger ones. Transportation of the groups to and from the theater was made easy by the fact that each school appeared only in the one episode.

The audience in any theater never realizes fully the hours of work and sacrifice that have gone into the finished product offered them. The most beautiful aspect of the pageant is the fact that, whereas professionals in the drama are paid and achieve fame for their labors, the amateurs who take part in a pageant sacrifice themselves for a cause, asking no monetary reward and content to be an insignificant unit in a great whole. As I watched the pageant "The Giant-Killer," I paid my honest tribute to the glorious, generous youth of America, and I was inspired with new hope for the future of American dramatic art. If one man can do all that Father Lord has done with the theater and with the young people of America, there is surely reason to believe that with united effort all of us who love dramatic art and sigh for its restoration to its glorious place as handmaid to religion, may at last redeem the American stage from its commercialized licentiousness and make of it the power for good that it was meant to be.

It does no good to tell young people or even old ones to stay away from the theater because it has become decadent. Our love for the drama is natural and it needs legitimate satisfaction. There is sound psychology back of the movement to put the drama again into the hands of the people, who demand, as they really have a right to demand, a substitute for the thing forbidden. Give the people their own drama, make it vital and interesting, and they will not feel the need to satisfy their instinct for drama among plays and players who will do them irreparable harm.

IX. THE PROMISE OF YOUNG AMERICA

IT was a beautiful pageant, a glamorous, colorful pageant of Youth. Were I to marshal all the glowing words that wrap their royal mantle round the long, sweet thoughts of life's springtime, I still should stand like a beggar at the roadside watching the king's cortège march into the distance, with no language to tell of his response to the golden shadow that touched his soul as the knightly host went by. There, before my suddenly misted eyes, fair Courtesy, that prince of graces, clothed itself in the uniform of an American soldier; assured Success reached out kindly hands to timid Aspiration; Youth, fine American Youth marched triumphantly to martial music.

Like figures in a dream they were; and yet in every young face was the dear familiar appearance of some American family likeness. Every straight boy in the cadet's uniform was somebody's son—somebody who squared his shoulders as John marched by, somebody who caught her breath at this passing Joe who had outgrown her tender arms. And the horses—were they real, or were they stolen perhaps from some dream-made Olympus where their dancing feet had been shod by a Vulcan in a merry humor? Never before had I seen horses dance as did these. Handsome bay horses danced on their slim, red-bound legs as they pulled rumbling cannons across the field. Gallant black horses, with their legs wrapped in white, danced under their riders, lovely, slim boys with eager faces lifted to the sun. And these young men and women walking sedately under banners—were they but the students who greeted us teachers daily in the dull setting of classrooms? No, there was more in this pageant than cadets and artillery and troops and students; the spirit of American youth incarnate paraded on that day across the sweet, sun-bathed grass.

The occasion was the Second Annual Indiana Literary Field Day, held at Culver Military Academy. There has never been much effort made to conceal the fact that Hoosiers are nothing at all if not enthusiastic about things Hoosier. As Meredith Nicholson said in his address on this day of May, 1926: "We Hoosiers would not for all the world have you think us conceited, but we are in duty bound to recognize our own possibilities and our own achievements." Indiana has set a precedent in the way of recognizing her distinguished sons and daughters and in the way of encouraging her boys and girls to develop their talents; and I am sure that all those who have been privileged to be at Culver for one of these occasions share the hope expressed by General L. R. Gignilliat, that this precedent may be followed by every state of the Union.

In accordance with the custom originated during the early months of 1925, the Indiana Literary League sends to the colleges and high schools of the State of Indiana invitations to enter a yearly contest. Cash prizes are offered for book illustrations, musical compositions, one-act plays, short stories, poems, and historical essays. These prizes are awarded at Culver Military Academy on Indiana Literary Day. The purpose of the contest is stated thus:

"The whole purpose of Literary Day centers on stimulating interest in literary and artistic endeavors by surrounding them with some of the sparkle and spangle and spirit that go with athletic contests. Rivalry has been introduced. Prizes are offered for the best work in state-wide competitions in poetry, book illustrating, the essay, the short story, and the one-act play. The

praises of the winners will be sung abroad. They
will be honored as are those heroes who score the
winning touchdowns. At this Hoosier Parnassus
the aspiring young poets and authors and artists
will be presented to the Literary Court of Honor.
Their colors will be flown from the tips of royal
pikes and they will be given a lift to at least one
step on the Ascent to Fame."

Every one who has been at Culver for a Literary Field Day feels that this admirable purpose
has been admirably achieved. I had the privilege
of being there on the second Field Day, and the
memory of it still abides fragrantly in my
thoughts. From ten in the morning till noon a
reception of guests was held in the recreation
building. Hospitality was perfect, beginning
when an officer in uniform met each party at the
station or at the automobile entrance, carried on
by every Culver man from General Gignilliat to
his youngest cadet, and ending only when hands
were waving in farewell. Because of the attentions showered upon our own particular party, we
felt that we must be the only guests of the occasion—until we discovered that we were of the
undistinguished multitude who were elevated to
distinction by the supreme solicitude of the as-
suredly distinguished.

After we had wandered through the Hoosier Salon of the Daughters of Indiana, which had temporary quarters in the gymnasium in order to display to good advantage Indiana's native talent on canvas, after we had sharpened our wits in the Literary Casino to discover the titles hidden in clever cartoons (there was, for example, a mournful hound with a lovelorn face, about whom exactly "Seventeen" fleas cavorted merrily), we went to join in the spectacular part of the day's program. A garrison parade formed in front of the recreation building and followed the band through a line of sentries to the grand stand on the field. There we saw young America in one of its finest manifestations: the drill of the cadets, the maneuvering of the artillery, the disciplining of the black horse troops, and the parade of students under their respective school colors.

As always there were present some of those dear blessed people who make themselves ridiculous for the common amusement. And there were reporters to tell us to "look pretty" and to photograph us to the utter satisfaction of the most vain. The young prize winner in our party told me she was simply devastated beyond repair by cameras— and she really ought not to mind having her picture taken.

A picnic luncheon was served in the gymnasium grove. This was all a picnic luncheon should be, with armies of ants demanding and securing their full share of the delicious viands on the festal board and with the accompanying music of the feast furnished in almost equal measure by the band and the mosquitoes. After the luncheon came the supreme hour for the prize winners. With all the pomp and splendor things military can give, Indiana's young artists and authors received their recognition from those competent to recognize them. Among the guests of honor were George Ade, Kin Hubbard, Chic Jackson, Harriet Monroe, Anna Nicholas, Richard H. Little, John T. McCutcheon, and Claude G. Bowers.

General Gignilliat made some introductory remarks, and then Meredith Nicholson, chairman of the League, paid tribute to the general for his great work in the upbuilding of the military academy. Mr. Nicholson called the roll of distinguished guests, introducing each of them. With the consummate tact of the successful artist who is thoroughly kind, he said graciously just the most encouraging thing about each of the younger artists whose success is not completely assured. With the freedom of a friendly man who scorns an accusation of flattery, he laid his tribute of praise at the feet of the deserving who have tasted the sweets of secure and enduring fame. Mr. Nicholson was followed on the program by Colonel George T. Buckingham of Chicago, past president of the Indiana Society of Chicago, who sang in genial way the praises of his native state and then thanked all those who had made the day possible.

Then, with a flare of drums and trumpets, with a military escort, under school colors flying from a royal pike, the proud young prize winners one by one mounted the steps and received their awards. Six times the gold and blue of Notre Dame and the blue and white of St. Mary's ascended the steps, and gladly I confess to having each time a genuine thrill of love and pride. The prize winners were presented to the guests of honor and received from them the friendly encouragement that means so much to the young.

The festivities continued into the evening, becoming altogether social at the end. The last strictly artistic events of the day were a handsome historical pageant and the presentation of the prize-winning play by the cadets. These being ended, the young people, having been furnished with a good orchestra, danced themselves to happy weariness.

Indiana has done a great and splendid thing in establishing this Literary Day. If only the other states will follow her example, we may have, on some memorable day, a National Literary Field Day. America is young. Not a century has elapsed since Europe wondered in idle moments whether anything good could ever come from this rude land of struggling pioneers whose hands seemed shaped for the plow rather than for the pen or the paint brush. Now, however, even old Europe with its crumbling cathedrals and its sacred traditions is beginning to see the romance that is America, to know that America is a land of promise unending, to discover that the young men and women of America do dream dreams and see visions that must be spun into the lovely stuff of poetry and splashed on canvas.

America is young, and so she has all the faults that belong to youth. But she has also the courage of youth and its dreams and aspirations that need courage for their fulfillment. She has the rash daring of youth that all too often brings disaster in its wake; for example, the rash daring of her young novelists who rush into political and moral and theological problems that their elders fear to enter. Richardson, Fielding, and Defoe were all over fifty years of age before they attempted

fiction; and they will still be stars in the literary
firmament when the candles of our young novelists have guttered in their sockets. Our young
poets would fain remake poetry; but the living
streams of song that flowed from Dante and
Shakespeare and Milton sweep serenely on, undis-
turbed by the futile hands that would stem them.
Youth is impatient of restraint and unreasonably
certain of its own unassailable rightness, and because of its impatience and its certainty of rightness it would break down conventions and creeds,
theories and principles, ideals and institutions that
happen to be in the way to what it considers its
privilege of self-realization. Literature is ever
the reflection of life; hence, in so much of our
contemporary literature, the absence of restraint,
the tearing aside of all decent reticences from matters once regarded as unmentionable, the revolt
against law and order, the free ridicule of those
who hold fast to creed and principle.

The pageantry of young America is a lovely
thing to behold when it is as I saw it on Culver's
field; for the cadets are boys who are taught religion, service, obedience, purity, and all other virtues that make for fine citizenship. It is a lovely
thing as I see it day after day in my own school;
for our girls are taught to be virtuous, God-

loving women who will bring beauty into the world they enter when they leave us. It is a lovely thing as I see it at the neighboring university, where hundreds of young men come every morning with hearts like Galahad's heart, freed from serious sin, to kneel at the white altar and receive the Bread of Life; for Notre Dame's glory is ever so much more in her daily communicants than in her football prowess. Youth is our treasure, indeed; and in the way of all treasures it needs careful guarding lest harm befall it. Youth will be lovely only so long as we who are older keep it so. There is a vast amount of fault being found with the younger generation, and most of us will admit that much of the fault-finding is justifiable. Surface fault-finding is, however, tragically easy, whereas probing for causes of faults is difficult. I do not think I am alone in believing that if we search deeply enough we shall find that most of what is wrong with the younger generation is also wrong with the older, in other, less obvious ways.

Countless numbers of young people to-day are being taught that there is no God. Shall we blame them, then, for knowing no morality? Without God as a lawgiver, right and wrong resolve into questions of social expediency or social custom.

Countless young people read lascivious books and attend immoral plays, and act in accordance with what they have learned from them; and their parents, who make no effort to suppress such books and plays, hold up their hands in horror at their sons' and daughters' first-hand knowledge of evil. Young people are allowed the utmost freedom in their search for pleasure; and yet, when they wreck themselves on the rocks of temptation, they are condemned pitilessly. Too much of our talking to young people nowadays is negative; we stress the "thou shalt not" rather than the "thou shalt." Instead of keeping their minds and hearts and bodies busy with worth-while work and amusement, we let them take their own ways; and then we wonder that they do not act as wisely as we should have done in their place. Rather than be forever at the business of berating the younger generation for its faults, we should learn its virtues and its possibilities and help to develop them. Looking for good qualities is an art practiced so infrequently that most of our abilities in that direction have grown rusty with disuse. Recognition of one's good qualities is an incentive to make sincere efforts to increase those good qualities. The Indiana Literary Field Day is a move in the right direction. The students gathered at Culver for these occasions receive far more than mere prizes for artistic and literary endeavor; they receive also the ennobling inspiration of a day in a place where the ideals of our pioneer ancestors are treasured as a sacred heritage, of a day in the company of men and women who have risen to greatness through courage and faith and endurance as well as through their God-given talents.

If it be true that Youth is failing American ideals, then it is also true that America has failed to set her ideals before the eyes of Youth. If children are trained in the way in which they should go, they do not as a rule depart from that way when they reach young manhood and womanhood. When we took God from our children by banishing Him from the schools, we prepared the way for the lack of faith and morality prevalent among the young to-day. History tells us that the wisest philosophers, when they were not fortified by revealed truth, made mistakes in their reasoning about God and morality. Can we, then, expect out children, untaught and alone, to grope their way to right standards of life? Can we wonder that a boy who knows nothing of the merciful forgiveness of God and the power of divine grace in the soul, on being brought face to

face with the shameful results of some dreadful
mistake on his own part, calmly sets a revolver
to his temple, to escape, in the endless sleep of
death, from the life that he feels is using him
cruelly? Why should we wonder that a girl who,
in the first place, has never been taught the intrinsic malice of sin and who, in the second, has
never had an opportunity to learn the story of
Christ and the Magdalen, should drink poison
to escape the censure of the world that will never
forgive her for her act of folly? When America
has thus failed Youth, shall she complain that
Youth is failing her?

We are rightly aggrieved at the frequent occur-
rence of drunkenness among the young to-day;
and yet surely we paved the way for it by an almost universal disregard of the prohibition law,
which was passed apparently for the sole purpose
of showing into what mockery the laws of our
nation may be turned. We are thoroughly dismayed at the immodest dress of our young women;
and yet from coast to coast the bodies of women
are exploited for the vicious, on the stage and
the screen and in bathing beauty contests. Mod-
esty is no inborn virtue; it is the result of training.
When the knees of little girls are exposed in socks
and short dresses till they reach their teens, one

cannot reasonably expect these girls suddenly to
develop a sense of impropriety in the revelation
of silk-clad knees after they reach their teens.
There are hundreds and hundreds of girls in this
country who simply do not understand that the
way in which they dress is a source of temptation
to men; for girls, unless taught otherwise, are
as a rule innocent of evil in their thoughts. I
know that what I have just said is true, because
I live in the closest hourly contact with dozens
and dozens of girls and have been the recipient
of innumerable confidences of an intimate kind. I
admit that our students are drawn from the better classes, a fact that in one way enhances the
value of my statement, because most of the disastrous licenses of young women to-day are to
be found among the better classes rather than
among the girls who must work for their liveli-
hood. I admit, too, with keenest joy, that our
girls have been trained in homes where God is
the unseen guest; and yet they are just as pleasure-
loving as are those girls who do not know the
meaning of moral restraint, and some of them,
moreover, need kind but firm discipline to keep
them from being extremists in dress and manner.
It is all too easy to throw the burden of our own
mistakes on the shoulders of our victims, a shift-

ing process that has been rather generously accomplished in this country of ours.

Youth of to-day is honest almost to unpardonable frankness; it is ambitious almost to utter selfishness; it is independent almost to revolt: but it seems to me a more hopeful characteristic to have virtues in excess rather than to suffer from inertia. There is much to admire in our young people of to-day and more reason for hope in them than for despair of them. It is essential, perhaps, to-day more than ever before, that we who have learned life's lessons awake to a deeper sense of the responsibility we have for those who are looking to us for guidance. Youth is a lovely, hopeful creature with dreams in its wistful eyes and with rainbow wings; and yet it is fatally easy for those eyes to become clouded and those wings to be bedraggled by the storms of life. The pageantry of American youth will be a glamorous, colorful thing of light and life and love, only so long as we who mark out its pathways see that they lead through clean, sweet, fruitful fields and that they do not enter the marsh of sensuality or the slough of despondency.

X. TRACKING THE HALF TRUTH

N the great open spaces of the American mind a prolific flock of half truths range at will. Theirs might be a safe and care-free existence were it not that occasionally zealous hunters after dangerous pests come into their midst and send them scurrying for cover to devious and darksome byways and to blind spots along the mental horizon. Hunting wary and elusive game is always good sport; and so I ask you to come with me on an expedition in which we shall hunt a few half truths to the death.

You know as well as I do that a great part of the world's moral blundering is due to these half truths. The whole-souled, honest-to-goodness lie is as sure as murder to come out from its hole, for it is a brazen creature prone to boast to passers-by of the ease with which some credulous person was fooled. The half truth, however, is a sly creature whose reminiscent smirk is of so doubtful character that it is often mistaken for the air of bashfulness. On this hunt we shall take with us the gentle hound of laughter, even though there will be serious situations and perhaps the tang of danger.

Among the half truths that have done irremediable harm of late is this one: the hereafter is a great uncharted adventure whereas life is rather dully prosaic. From harboring this half truth too long a noteworthy number of young people have committed suicide. Another dangerous half truth is that marriage often proves cruelly disappointing. This half truth has carried a lamentable number of marriages into the divorce court, wherein personal selfishness is euphoniously labeled incompatibility. Another half truth is that large families often entail what seem like unendurable difficulties and sacrifices. From meditating on this half truth the classes of society who could most easily take care of large families are limiting the number of their children.

The particular half truth I want now to track to death has to do with the theory that the higher education of woman is one of the primary causes of the decay of the American home, a cause vitally connected with the three pernicious evils I have just mentioned. Since I shall be pursuing my half truth in the approved manner of the

propagandist, you may, perhaps, be asked to perform some startling gymnastic stunts in reasoning.

Most of us, even those with least agility in pre-
varication, will grant when pushed to it that
woman determines in large measure the social and
moral stability of the world. To-day two facts
are outstanding: a great number of women go to
college; the world is going wrong. By a simple
process of adding these facts we may conclude
that the strongest motive force among those
freely and openly pushing the world of to-day on
its toboggan ride down the hill of destruction
is the higher education of woman. Thus I have
been precipitated into my thesis, which is, that
the higher education of woman is unsafe, because
it unfits her for her natural part in the work of
guiding the world aright.

The first task in the proper support of any
thesis is explanation of its terms. What, then,
do we mean by the higher education of woman?
We mean not merely education from the eyebrows
up but development of the whole woman, physical,
mental, and moral, by a sane, sound, college training. What do we mean by woman's natural part
in the work of guiding the world aright? Gentle
reader, put on your cap and bells, and, after the

delightful French, *"Marchons!"* Some few benighted survivors of the medieval intellectuals tell
us that woman's natural work is to be the inspiration of man, the maker of the home, and the real,
helpful mother of a family. Let us, for the moment, grant the truth of this preposterously
gratuitous assumption and consider the higher
education of woman in regard to it.

If we grant this assumption we must grant also
certain corollaries of it. To be the inspiration
of man, the home-maker, and the guide of her
children, woman must possess certain qualities
and characteristics. She must be beautiful, submissive, industrious, and, if we be of medieval
prepossessions, religious. One might add intelligent, but that would be begging the question involved in our thesis. Besides, there can not be
true congenial contentment in the home where
the wife is educated to any marked degree of intelligence. Woman's mind is supposed to be the
placid, docile, and, above all, empty receptacle
into which masculine oratory can be freely poured.
Now, imagine the legitimate consternation of a
husband who tries to pour facts, or his interpretation of facts, into a mind already filled with facts.
The retort, as in a well-filled bottle of wine, is
bound to be forthcoming. As for submissiveness,

obviously a woman with intelligent opinions of her own will not be unquestioningly submissive to all the caprices of masculine wisdom, even if it be her husband's wisdom. It is small wonder that divorce on grounds of incompatibility is so very frequent nowadays; for is not feminine resistance to masculine judgment the man's definition of incompatibility?

Hence, without more ado, we strike out intelligence from the list of requisites for the woman who is going to perform her part in the work of the world. If we wished to dwell on this subject we might remark that though Pericles had his Aspasia, Dante his Beatrice, Petrarch his Laura, and Boccaccio his Fiametta—it is best to draw our examples from a more romantic past—we have no record of the intelligence, real or alleged, of these women, and no evidence that in any of these cases the great man was wedded to the lady of his predilection. Excellent use is being made of this half truth to-day. Husbands and wives must be inspired somehow to "realize their finer selves," and they cannot find such inspiration at home, it seems. Life at home seems indeed "flat, stale, and unprofitable." The wife of the actor who makes feminine hearts flutter must needs seek *her* heart-fluttering from some other source. We wander. Half truths furnish all too many opportunities for detours.

Woman must be beautiful, even if not intelligent. Let us go carefully. Can there be true beauty and inspiration in eyes with lines between them, tortoise-shell spectacles athwart them, and keen scrutiny behind them? Yet, if we may judge by appearances, these death dealers to beauty are almost inevitable concomitants of a bachelor's degree. Surely this is the real argument against the higher education of woman. Nor is this all. College women, having become possessed of the idea that beauty of face is perhaps of less significance than beauty of mind and soul, may in one instance or another continue their efforts to acquire knowledge, even after the door of their Alma Mater has clanged behind them. Imagine a woman who greets her husband with her face shining, as a result of having read Dante again on a rainy afternoon, after a habit of school days. In the face of the fact that she forgot her powder could any man be expected to know that the eyes of her soul are shining because they have been looking on the effulgent light of the Mystic Rose? No, woman cannot be both beautiful and educated, and she must be beautiful. The conclusion is obvious.

Until comparatively recent times the acquisition of a husband meant to a woman also a home and motherhood. We have outgrown this primitive notion; but, having made certain assumptions in the beginning of this argument, I must, in order to be consistent, consider the relation of the higher education of woman to the home and motherhood. If college does nothing else for the student, it at least teaches her the value of methodical use of time and the need of industry for achievement. In the old-fashioned home time was an asset; but time spent in the home nowadays is accounted a dead loss. Hence, college education utterly unfits the modern woman for the home in this respect as well as in regard to industry. Why should women be industrious when there are husbands willing to pay salaries to maids? As for children —poor old Malthus, were he alive to-day, would be shouting from the housetops that the millennium is here and would advocate the further multiplication of kennels. Dear little pomeranians and poodles and chows, how these would delight his heart! Of course, there are some homes with children in them; and we must consider the higher education of woman in regard to these barbarous vestiges of an older civilization and less modern morality. Does a college education make a woman less the mother? I shall, in the manner of my race, answer this question by asking questions. Should a mother investigate the merits of the teachers of her children? Should a mother tell her children what to read? Should she study their lessons with them? Should she be able to meet her college son on his own ground with arguments to prove the duty he has to live whether he likes life or not?

Having been almost ultra-medieval in handling my thesis, let me approach the limit itself, and mention that last word in medievalism, the college with religious instruction in its curriculum. What can be more harmful to progress in the days of *This Freedom* than to teach woman that she is to worship an obsolete God, to teach her that she should observe moral and civil law, to teach her that vows are sacred and binding? Such teaching is bound to counteract the up-to-date lesson of "A Doll's House." Nora must "realize herself"; and the city streets at night are a more effective place for such realization than is a home with a husband and three or four children. The college with religious instruction in its curriculum is prone to make women too shy of city streets at night for genuine self-realization thereon. Not all the obstacles in the way of woman's freedom can be laid at the door of colleges, however. In fact, I know of several women who had only a grade of high school education who have lived with their husbands during many years and have brought up fine sons and daughters. And I have yet to hear any of them complain that she never had a chance to "realize herself." Most of them were so busy and happy in being good wives and mothers that they seldom gave themselves a thought. They should now be ashamed of their unrealized state, when self-realization drives multitudes of other women to the psychoanalyst.

In attempting to prove my thesis I asked you to grant an assumption. Now, after the manner of the economists, I shall remind you that the assumption holds only in the hypothetical world wherein woman is really the inspirer of men, the maker of the home, and the helpful mother of children. As to its validity in this world of ours, opinions may differ. Because my serious opinion is that women can fulfill these duties in this world of ours and because my firm belief is that the saving of the world from destruction is largely in the hands of women and because I am hopelessly medieval, I do my best to teach the young women in our college to be beautiful of mind and soul and exquisite of body, to be submissive to proper authority, to regard human life in even its earliest stages sacred, to be industrious, to be religious, yes, even to be intelligent; for I feel that thus they will be better fitted for their natural part in the work of the world. And I go further: I even tell them that it is their duty to use their suffrage in helping to direct the affairs of the nation, though this may add another to their problems of marital adjustment and furnish another reason for so-called incompatibility.

There is much talking and writing nowadays about the supposed antagonism between the sexes. A great part of the opinions are expressed by callow young men and smart girls, and they foreshadow the later "incompatibilities" of the divorce court. Not long ago a college man gave forth what must have seemed to him a clever remark to the effect that woman is inferior to man for the reason that she was made from man's rib. A girl of mental height equal to his retorted that man was made from slime and so woman seemed to have the better of material. Any decent adult resents this flippant repartee. If such a young man deserved an answer at all, the answer should have been, "Never was there a man so degraded as not to exult lovingly in the fact that he was fashioned blood and flesh and bone from the blood and flesh and bone of the finest woman he knows, and because he was thus fashioned he exalts that woman to a pedestal before which he kneels." The sexes were made by God to complement each other, and there can be no question of anything but a relative superiority of one over the other. Each sex has its own superiorities and inferiorities to the other. Because of the superiorities we respect and need each other; because of the inferiorities we love and help each other. The higher education of both men and women should but drive home these truths and make each sex more thoughtful of the other; and so one can but become impatient when silly young persons air their "antagonisms" and their "incompatibilities" to the world.

Higher education should do much to drive all half truths from our minds. Where it is possible we should laugh them to death, for no pompous theory can long survive the steady onslaught of laughter. Dozens of our magazine writers and our teachers of to-day are advancing against good things arguments as silly as the one I have just concluded, against the higher education of woman. They argue God from His universe, man from his place as lord of creation, a place that is his by right of his reason; they argue souls from our bodies, eternity from our God-given vision, and morality from our words and actions; and their arguments are made up of half truths that are more dangerous than outright lies. Half truths are dangerous and fascinating because of the very element of truth in them. Perhaps the most devastating of the half truths we are told to-day is the slogan that Christianity has failed. The whole truth is that as a people we have not even given Christianity a chance to fail or to win. Given any chance whatsoever Christianity wins in the case of the individual; and there is no reason to think that it could not win in the case of the nation, which is, after all, only a group of individuals. On this slogan, it seems to me, is reared the whole fabric of half truths that are destroying the morality of the world to-day. Christianity, and it alone, can give the death blow to every kind of lie.

A believing Christian, for example, understands that perfect happiness is impossible in this world, for the reason that it is reserved for the life to come, and yet he would never end his life in the hope of securing that happiness more quickly. No matter how poor and sick and unhappy the Christian may be, he does not lose hope. Pessimists who prate of human misery surely do not know the fact of Christian fortitude in the face of misery, a fortitude made possible by the belief that pain in this life may be used to purchase bliss in the next. Christians have a right sense of values, and so they reason that the loss of every human joy matters not at all if the soul be well in God's sight. Christ established the correct sense of values for us all when, dying in utter disgrace and loneliness and pain, He saw in the face of a wretched thief that His sacrifice was worth while.

XI. HOSPITALS FOR THE HOPELESSLY HEALTHY

BEING an insignificant twig on the family tree of which Mark Twain is the most illustrous branch, having in me a slight strain of Quaker and a large element of Irish, and being a native-born Hoosier, I am naturally one of those in some ways unfortunate persons who have irresistible desires to laugh at the wrong time. When everything else in me is laughing that Quaker strain lifts its immaculate hands in horror, and then I am forced to ask myself as Alice asked the Gnat when she saw two large tears roll from its eyes, "Why do you make jokes if it makes you so unhappy?"

Now I might have added that the religious dignity belonging to me as a nun also protests against unseemly levity; but many nuns will read this book, and that statement, plausible as it sounds, would be challenged by every one of them. Nuns have caught the whole secret of joyous laughter and hidden it safe behind demure scapulars. Not without reason is the novice in religious life defined as one who breaks crockery and giggles. Why should there not be laughter in the heart of the bride of God? Blessed Jordan of Saxony knew what he was talking about when he told his novices: "Laugh to your hearts' content, my dearest children . . . It is only right that you should laugh after breaking from the devil's thraldom . . . Laugh on, then, and be as merry as you please, my darling sons."

Added to all these inherited tendencies was a youth spent in large measure in an inland lake or on a horse or wherever anything athletic was happening. Hence, how unutterably funny to me are deliberately indoor, stuffy people, will be easily understood. Whenever I drive through the grounds of the University of Notre Dame and see several hundred young men chasing a football on the practice field, I begin to wonder frivolously just what the author of *A Connecticut Yankee at King Arthur's Court* could have done with a knight of that court on a football field in our steam-heated America. Suppose the knight should land in New York City and form his impressions of American youth in cabarets and such places and then, with these impressions, should journey to the field on which Knute Rockne is king, he would, doubtless, reason in some such fashion as this:

Ours is the golden age of boastful unhealthiness. The spirit of the times is evidenced by our very manner of salutation, the inevitable "How are you?" This question almost invariably evokes a detailed account of the multifarious miseries of ill-being. The one who responds to this inquiry with a hearty "Tip-top" usually causes surprise, disappointment, even disgust. If the unfortunate possessor of health add to this eccentricity a calloused indifference to our gratuitous tale of woe, he soon becomes a pariah, an outcast unworthy of fellowship in our anemic, lachrymose generation. Contrasts of the kind afforded by his zest of living are odious and intolerable. Hence, all those hopelessly healthy persons, who refuse to conform to the spirit of the age, who habitually insist upon being well, should, lest they spread their pernicious ideas, be segregated into well isolated hospitals. They are a standing reproach, a constant menace to the morale of our young men of flat chests and our young women of the "débutante slouch." Away with them into remote isolation where there may be created for them the rude atmosphere of the Middle Ages! Our steam-heated generation would have none of them.

The disease of healthiness in its fullest development creates a surplus energy which often drives the victim into an orgy of athletic exercise. Certain kinds of such exercise show that the malady is very contagious, though the effects of the contagion are manifested rather in the inducement of vicarious suffering than in the implanting of the germs of the disease itself. By no species of such exercise is this peculiar effect of borrowed agony so fatally induced as by the game of football, a survival of medieval barbarism still promoted at some of our modern universities. Truly, there is little hope for us if we cannot make those whose task it is to preside over the activities of our young people see the necessity of barring from our schools every young man with a football physique?

What is higher education for? Surely it has nothing to do with football. Surely the impressionability of the interior of a young man's head is more important in an entrance examination than the unimpressionability of his head's exterior. Yet the man whose cranium has the resistance of a goat's, whose arms have the grip of a bear's, and whose legs have the speed of a deer's, usually wins more prestige among his fellows than does the future valedictorian.

The press is doing little to stem the spread of this malady of heartiness; sometimes it even lends itself to the promulgation of heretical ideas concerning it. As an instance of this evil propaganda we may note here that some press notices concerning the football prowess of a certain middlewestern university stated in glowing terms that the "Irish" team idolized by this particular university played football "from the shoulders up." We are still puzzling over the meaning of the encomium as applied to a game requiring such agility of the lower extremities of the athletes, though we were told it has something to do with united efforts on the part of the team.

For no other reason in the world except our distress over the danger that is threatening us from the disease of healthiness we recently interviewed a scholarly friend of ours who had in a moment of folly attended a football game and had as a result become slightly insane on the subject. We thought that if we should study the symptoms of the malady in its earlier stages we might be able to discover some effective remedy. Sad to relate, we almost caught the contagion ourselves. We slept for a few nights with our windows open wider than usual. The malady increased. Then we slept for a few nights with our windows tightly closed and thus killed all the germs. Our inborn fear of night air was en-

larged recently by a brutal person who remarked:
"You shut your windows because night air is unhealthy. Just what kind of air do you breathe
at night if not night air?" After hearing this we
stayed awake several nights worrying. Really,
it was asking too much of even us to require that
we hold our breath during nine hours.

Our friend gave us this account of his experience at the football game. For a good three
hours he sat with some thousands of others on a
wind-swept set of bleachers in a cold drizzling
rain and watched—not in appropriately silent
mourning but in a sort of noisy delirious ecstasy—
twenty-two young victims of a dreadful disease
engaged in what appeared to be a struggle to the
death. Though it was in divers respects a grim
and fearful spectacle, the band played madly during the intervals while the athletes rested, and the
student body yelled vociferously, as one voice,
certain strange cheers usually terminating with the
name of some especially violent sufferer from the
malady. Whenever one of the athletes was
"knocked out," as they call it, flat upon the field,
the spectators in frenzied fashion besought him
to get up and renew his struggle. Such heartless-
ness our friend had never seen before; and he re-
solved firmly not to repeat his investigation into

this virulent manifestation of the plague—at least not until the next October, when he would have had time to recover from the shock to his nerves.

Beside our friend on the uncomfortable bleacher was a short-sighted, round-shouldered boy of some nineteen years, an apparently ideal student, who, unfortunately having swallowed a germ, actually went raving mad during the game. He was and forever shall be a stranger to our friend; yet he howled in his ear, pounded him on the back, trampled on his feet, fell upon his neck, and embraced him hysterically. No one, it seems, is immune to the contagion. On the other side of our friend was a girl; in truth, he had brought her to the game. She was scantily clad, after the manner of girls. This young woman, who, as the teacher of physical culture in her college testifies, shivers and gasps her refusal on the plea of danger to health when the students take a two-mile hike on a clear day, sat there in the cold rain, or rather jumped up and down beside our friend and shivered, it seemed, only in the ecstasy of enthusiasm. Because our scholarly friend likes this young woman, he refrained from caustic comments on feminine inconsistency and contented himself with gazing sadly about him—when he could distract his attention from the awful scene on the field before him. The sadness in his gaze may have had something to do with the fact that the young woman called him some such name as boob because he was not more enthusiastic.

There on the bleachers about our friend were hundreds of young men and women in gala attire, whose personal use for athletic apparel obviously can but be forever unheralded and unsung, straining their nerves, muscles, and voices, while they suffered vicariously with the twenty-two savages chasing and pummeling one another. Suddenly our friend caught the malady. He wept in anguish when the eleven young men whom he really loves seemed to be fighting a losing game. He hated the other eleven men venomously. His hate turned to pity, however, when they were swept to ignominious defeat. Obviously, such harrowing of emotions could but have disastrous effects; he was, as a matter of brute fact, unable to speak above a whisper for two days thereafter.

Again we plead that young men such as those of the gridiron be segregated into hospitals for the purpose, even if it be necessary to have a stadium attached. Let us send with them all the fresh-air fiends, the golfers, the horseback riders, and, particularly, those who usurp the prerogatives of the long-suffering fishes. These miserable individuals are spreading contagion far and wide, and if we do not take timely measures against them we shall all become victims of their malady. What, then, will our doctors, our sanatorium managers, and our manufacturers of cosmetics do for a living? What will become of our street corner salesmen of patent medicines? What will our directors of beauty parlors do? These are questions that cry to the heavens for answer.

Now, if our knight of King Arthur's court should, after the manner of the immortal Don Quixote, take it upon himself to ride from the stadium of one of our great universities to another and deliver the foregoing oration to the athletes, or if he should mimeograph these remarks and send them as a sort of open letter to the football coaches of the United States of America, I think the reactions of those lusty gentlemen would be somewhat interesting. But I think the effect of the letter might be even more interesting if these same football coaches, who are, as a rule, gentlemanly in many senses, should be informed of the fact that the writer is of the sex that dares to talk at random with impunity.

XII. THE CASE FOR THE PAROCHIAL SCHOOL

ATHOLICS seem to be at their best when the storms of persecution are raging about them. They appreciate their Catholic privileges more fully when those privileges are attacked. In this way they are but human. No matter, for example, how indifferent Catholics throughout the country are toward their parochial school system; no matter how much they are attracted to the public school because of its supposed social or educational advantages—Catholics throughout the country come to the immediate defense of their school system the moment it seems to be in danger. I am sure, however, that a noteworthy percentage of these Catholics, along with the Protestants, are wondering in their hearts just why bishops and priests and religious teachers and enlightened laymen insist on the attendance of Catholic children at the parochial school.

It is a fact that many of our Catholic people have but one reason for sending their children to the parochial school, and that reason is, they are commanded to do so by the Church. That it might be a patriotic duty never enters their minds. Yet it is such a duty. Catholic educators have been so busy in trying to keep the parochial schools in existence and to maintain them on a high level of excellence that they have had no time to explain the mechanism of the parochial school system, by which religion permeates all instruction during the plastic and formative years of the child's life and gives him a character equal to the demands of Christian living in society. If the principles of the Catholic school system were understood it would not have to stay on the defensive. It would receive ardent support from people of all faiths if they understood more fully the reason for its existence. The Catholic school system is one of America's strongest bulwarks against all the forces that make for disintegration of the nation.

The school is of course a social institution. Like any social institution, then, it proves its right to existence by its services to society, its history, its intrinsic excellence, and its expediency. I shall attempt to show that the parochial school system is of almost inestimable service to society, that it is justified by its history, that it is in itself excellent, and that it is the most practical and expedient school system in the country.

The Oregon school bill was defeated on the principle that the parent and not the state has the right to educate the child. This is a Christian principle, and any denial of it is a reversion to paganism. In pagan Greece Plato wrote his *Republic* to describe his ideal, the communistic state. In this state there was community of children as well as of goods. Children unfit for military or other public service were left to die on the hills, and the remaining children, kept in public nurseries after separation from their parents, belonged to the state. In pagan Rome children unfit for military service or for agricultural pursuits were left on the hills to die by parents who thus performed a patriotic duty. In heathen China superfluous baby girls are fed to the beasts of the forests, because only male children can offer worship to the shades of their ancestors and carry on the work of the nation. These monstrous things were conceived in the name of patriotism.

Though we of Christian America went to war in the sacred name of Democracy, we set limits to the demands of patriotism. We understand democracy to mean that the state exists for the individual and not that the individual exists for the state. We believe that the state is builded on the individual and that it must protect his rights. This belief our forefathers wrote into the Declaration of Independence. We maintain that "absolute and arbitrary power over the lives, liberty, and property of free men exists nowhere in a Republic, not even in the largest majority," as the Kentuckians put it in their Constitution of 1850. These same Kentuckians in 1891 added the following amendment to the section on religious liberty of their Bill of Rights: "nor shall any man be compelled to send his child to any school to which he may be conscientiously opposed." On just this principle was the notorious Oregon bill defeated.

Now, how does the Catholic school system serve society? First, we must get rid of any foolish notion that Catholicism is opposed to Americanism. Catholics accept very literally the words of St. Paul: "Let every soul be subject to higher powers: for there is no power but from God: and those that are, are ordained of God. Therefore he that resisteth the power, resisteth the ordinance of God. And they that resist, purchase to themselves damnation." Therefore Catholics can but endorse heartily this dictum from the Supreme Court of Pennsylvania in the case of Updegraph vs. the Commonwealth: "Christianity is part of the common law of this state. . . . Its foundations are broad and strong and deep; they are laid in the authority, the interest, the affections of the people. Waiving all question of hereafter, it is the purest system of morality, the finest auxiliary, the only stable support of all human laws."

Catholics can but endorse also the words of President Coolidge in a letter to Dr. James E. Freeman, Bishop of the Protestant Episcopal diocese of Washington: "Whatever inspires and strengthens the religious activities of the people, whatever ministers to their spiritual life, is of supreme importance. Without it all other efforts will fail. With it there lies the only hope for success. The strength of our country is the strength of its religious convictions." Catholics can but recall with pride the third article of the Northwest Ordinance, adopted by the Congress of the Confederation in 1787: "Religion, morality, and knowledge being necessary to good government and the happiness of mankind, schools and the means of education shall be forever encouraged." Finally, Catholics can but hearken with misgiving to the indictment of the public schools uttered by Dr. Eliot in Boston on December 9,

1922: "The failure of our public schools to turn out good citizens and good voters is conspicuous. We shall have to look it squarely in the face. First teach children their duty to parents, brothers and sisters. Children in the public schools are getting nothing of it at this moment. Many of them are getting nothing of it at home. Teach the meaning of loving their neighbors. Beyond that is the motive of putting into children's hearts the love of God."

These statements carry with them the weight of conviction. Now, what have they to do with the Catholic school? The Catholic point of view in regard to the relation between religion and citizenship is set forth in the 1919 Pastoral of the American Hierarchy published by the National Catholic Welfare Conference: "Since the child is a member not only of the family, but also of the larger social group, his education must prepare him to fulfil his obligations to society. The community has the right to insist that those who, as members, share in its benefits shall possess the necessary qualifications. The school, therefore, whether private or public as regards maintenance and control, is an agency for social welfare, and as such it bears responsibility to the whole civic body. While the social aspect of education is evidently important, it must be remembered that social righteousness depends upon individual morality. . . . For this very reason the attempt to develop the qualities of citizenship without regard for personal virtue, or to make civic utility the *one* standard of moral excellence is doomed to failure. Integrity of life in each citizen is the only guarantee of worthy citizenship." These are plain words and true.

Dr. John A. Lapp in *The Catholic Citizen* further elucidates the Catholic point of view: "The objectives in teaching American citizenship are: to impart the knowledge of American democracy and government which the citizen needs to have; to implant moral ideals for the guidance of community action; to give an understanding of civic rights; and to imbue the citizen with a passionate desire to perform his civic duties with ability and honor."

Teachers in Catholics schools are able to prepare their children for their duties as citizens because they understand that good citizenship depends on individual Christian morality. This preparation for citizenship is one of the most important services rendered to society by the parochial school system. If it did no more than this, its reason for existence would be justified.

In what does this preparation for citizenship consist? Believing that life is a training school for eternity, that right living requires religious preparation, that individual and social conduct is governed by right standards of morality, the Catholic school endeavors to develop the whole child, physically, mentally, and morally, to train the heart as well as the head of the student, to give him something more than education from the eyebrows up. The Catholic school endeavors to teach the true meaning of liberty as opposed to license, to teach that liberty means the freedom to develop all one's rights without unreasonable hindrance and without trespassing on the rights of others. Just this and nothing more. The Catholic school endeavors to implant in the child respect for himself, his home, his country, and his God. If a child is trained to obey the Ten Commandments of God, he must respect the rights of others; he can but be a law-abiding citizen. Hence the upholder of the nation should uphold also the Catholic school.

The Catholic school system is, moreover, historically justified. It is a truism that history and product are two proofs of the worth or the worthlessness of an institution. No Catholic need ever fear to appeal to these proofs in justification of the school system he calls his own.

All the schools in the Colonial period, whether established by Catholics or Protestants, were religious schools; and there were no state schools, supported by public taxation. In establishing their own schools Catholics were but doing as all colonists did. The development of Catholic schools has been normal, proportional to the increase in the Catholic population. Yet Protestants as well as Catholics, Jews, Mongolians, Latins, Slavs, Teutons, Negroes, poor and rich, clever and dull—all have been gathered within the walls of the Catholic school. The statistics of enrollment in any Catholic school show that there is nothing exclusive in the membership; and therefore to this school belongs also the advantage claimed particularly for the public school, the rubbing shoulders of the common lot, the boiling in the American melting pot. Catholic schools are democratic schools, because they are schools of a democracy. Catholic schools are schools in which religion is taught, because they are the schools of a country which professes to worship God and the schools of a people whose religion is the corner stone whereon is builded their virtue as individual citizens of a country dearer to them than life. All that Catholics ask of their country is the right to the souls of their own children; and this is a small request in free America, though it might have been a great request in Cæsar-ridden Rome.

The very word Catholic is almost synonymous with patriotism. Catholics love their country, and they willingly gave more than their share of the boys who went overseas. These boys were the product of the parochial schools of the United States, and they seem to have been just as good targets for enemy guns as the other boys in our army. Is not this the supreme test of patriotism? Catholics in the World War gave freely as did the Catholics of the Revolutionary War, to whom Washington said in his speech given in December, 1779: "I presume that your fellow citizens will not forget the patriotic part which you took in the accomplishment of their revolution and the establishment of their government, or the important assistance which they received from a nation in which the Roman Catholic Religion is professed."

To any fair-minded searcher into its records, the Catholic school is proved by its services to society and its history to be an American institution of unmistakable worth as a means of training for citizenship. Its intrinsic excellence as an educational factor is no less unmistakable. Its expediency ought to appeal to us Americans because of our business acumen. The very reason for the excellence of the parochial school system is also the reason for its social expediency. I refer to its teaching body, composed in great part of the Catholic Sisterhoods of the country. Though the Catholic school boasts its equality in educational matters with the public school, it makes no claim to superiority—save only perhaps in the devotedness and stability of its teaching body. It does justly claim a more painstaking care of the child's soul than is afforded by the public school.

The question of the social expediency of the Catholic school involves us in a practical, financial issue. Statistics are always useful to the person of practical mind. I gathered statistics concerning the Catholic schools in the archdioceses of Baltimore, Chicago, Cincinnati, Dubuque, Milwaukee, New York City, Philadelphia, St. Louis, San Francisco, and St. Paul. These statistics show that the Catholics in these ten fairly representative districts of our country support at present 1,698 schools in which 562,733 children are taught. The salaries for teachers alone in these districts would be staggering figures were the state compelled to pay them. Attributing 40 children to a teacher, the state would have to provide 14,068 grade instructors. At a conservative estimate, a yearly salary of $900.00 would have to be paid to every teacher. This would mean an annual drain of $12,661,200.00 additional taxes from the people of these ten districts merely to pay the added force of instructors. Then these districts would be compelled either to buy the schools already in existence or to build and equip 1,698 schools, for the reason that the public grade schools of these districts are filled to overflowing.

In a bulletin "A Catechism of Catholic Education," published in 1920 by the National Catholic Welfare Conference, there are some statistics which will throw further light on this problem. In the year 1920 the states of this country paid $950,000,000.00 for the education of 23,250,000 children in elementary schools. This means that it costs approximately $40.00 to educate one child during one year in the public schools. Exclusive, then, of buildings and equipment, the bill to educate the 2,000,000 Catholic children would be $80,000,000.00 annually. It may therefore in fairness be said that the Catholics of the United States make an annual contribution to public education of this huge sum, which would represent the annual interest at 5 per cent on a capital of

$1,600,000,000.00. This does not include the costs of buildings and equipment, which would be approximately $288,000,000.00. Surely it is socially expedient for the United States to have within the country a group of people who not only support the public schools by taxes, but also save the nation, by maintaining private schools, such a huge expenditure. The reason why Catholics are willing to bear this burden is the simple one that they wish the religion and morals of their children to be safeguarded.

Exact statistics are not available as to the average cost of maintenance of pupils in Catholic schools, but it seems to be between one-third and one-half the cost of maintenance of pupils in the public schools. The salaries paid to teachers are a large item in the reduction in cost in the parochial school. The teaching Sisters in this country receive on an average $300.00 a year as salary. One may well ask, How do they manage to live? And one may answer, Very poorly. Yet we must reckon with the fact that Sisters can live more cheaply than other teachers. Though they equip their schools according to highest standards, personally they live in a voluntary poverty at which the world may well wonder. Take, for example, the Sister's bill for clothes. She gets a new dress, or habit, once in about five years. This habit, which she makes for herself, costs about $18.00. Just set this item over against one fur coat. Sisters are served at table with good, plain food, which, being purchased in large quantities, makes an inexpensive menu. In a Sister's bedroom there are an iron bed, a chair or two, a stand, and a small wardrobe. There is no carpet on the floor. Therefore it costs little to support a Sister, so little, in fact, that most Sisters work for far less than a living wage. Those who know anything at all about Sisters know that in some poor missions the Sisters lack even necessities.

The motive power that can draw women from homes of love and often of luxury to lives of such self-denial is obviously spiritual. They hear and accept in their literal meaning the words of the divine Master, "Sell all whatever thou hast, and give to the poor, and thou shalt have treasure in heaven: and come, follow me." They leave all that life has to give, take unto themselves voluntary vows of poverty, chastity, and obedience, and devote their lives to the teaching of children. With practically nothing to distract their attention from their profession and with every incentive to perfect themselves in it, they can but become real teachers in every sense of the term. What can the Republic not hope from such women as they? Are not women who have given their whole lives to the profession of teaching more likely to be good teachers than girls who teach during the interval between school and marriage for the sake of earning more spending money than their fathers can give them? I have nothing but happy memories of my own public school training, and so I have no quarrel to pick with the public school—except the recent movement to make the public school not only nonreligious but irreligious as well. Yet I do ask that the teaching Sisterhoods of this country be given their just dues and be evaluated at their true worth.

Henry Clay is a great man in American history. Though not a Catholic, he was big enough to understand a religious vocation. When his granddaughter was about to enter a convent he wrote to her: "While we could not disapprove, we were seriously and sorrowfully concerned by your resolution to adopt the veil and dedicate the rest of your life to the service of God in a convent. We could not disapprove because you say that your determination had been deliberately formed and because you are solemnly convinced that it will be conducive to your present and future happiness. . . . I have no prejudice against the Catholic religion. On the contrary, I sincerely believe that Catholics, who are truly religious, are as sure of happiness in another world as the most pious Protestants. . . . Adieu, my dear grandchild, may God enlighten, guide, and direct you; and if we never meet again in this world may we meet in the regions of eternity and there join my beloved daughter, your lamented mother. Such also are the prayers of your grandma." The nun did well to treasure such a letter for us to read in these days when our convents are so vilified by the scurrilous writings of obscene pens.

Thomas Jefferson, another man of whom all Americans are proud, wrote in July, 1794, to the superior of the Ursuline nuns in Louisiana: "I have received, Holy Sisters, the letters you have written to me, wherein you express anxiety for the property invested in your institution by the former Government of Louisiana. The principles of the Constitution of the United States are a sure guarantee that it will be preserved to you sacred and inviolate. . . . Whatever diversity of shade may appear in the religious opinions of our fellow-citizens, the charitable objects of your institution can not be indifferent to any; and its furtherance of the wholesome purposes of society by training up its young members in the way they should go, can not fail to insure it the patronage of the Government it is under. Be assured it will meet with all the protection my office can give it."

The Ursulines were reassured by President Madison in his turn: "In a country where all rights, religious as well as civic, are protected by the laws, and guaranteed by an enlightened public opinion, the best of securities exists for the tranquility and esteem of those whose labors are devoted to the conscientious pursuits of laudable objects. It remains only, therefore, to insure you that however inferior to my predecessor in other merits, my dispositions are equally friendly to the task of training youth in the paths of virtue, and useful knowledge, and that with my thanks for the prayers of your religious community, I offer mine, for the happiness of the members composing it."

It is consoling to consider that the principles of these men and of our constitution were upheld by the Supreme Court of the United States when the Oregon school bill was on trial. These three great Americans, Clay, Jefferson, and Madison understood America and her ideals; they read aright her motto, "Liberty, Equality, Fraternity";

they respected her democracy; they realized that the state exists for the individual and must safeguard all his rights; they could not understand unreasoning prejudice; they were big of mind and heart just because they were real Americans. They understood that religion is an essential part of all education and that religious men and women, of all teachers in the world, are best prepared to permeate education with religion, and thus to make their students into good citizens of the commonwealth. Those train best for time who train for eternity. Training for eternity is the primary purpose of the Catholic school, and therefore it is best able to perform also the secondary purpose, training the whole child for his life's work in the world.

XIII. INTRODUCING THE CHILDREN TO THE SAINTS

THERE is only one thing in literature more entrancing to children than the fairy tale, and that is the story of a saint. By children I mean not only those under fifteen years of age but also those blessed persons who never become so unfortunate as to "grow up," even after they have passed the allotted decades of man. If stress of duties permit me the privilege of reading daily for a half hour from the lives of the saints, I shall still be very young when I celebrate my ninetieth birthday, whether I be then in the body or out of it.

If any two classes of people deserve to be introduced to each other, they are children and the saints of God. Wordsworth was, I think, writing more than pretty verse when he said that "trailing clouds of glory do we come from God, who is our home." About the head of every unspoiled child is a glorious veil of innocence. About the head of every saint is this same cloud of glory, preserved, or recovered through loving penance. Children see the world through a rosy mist of

imagination and idealism. Saints also see the
world through a rosy mist, such a mist as per-
chance hovered over the deep when the Spirit of
God moved across the waters, bringing light that
heralded sun and moon and stars, a mist so beautiful that the God who made it said that it was
good. Children idealize their parents because
they love them. Saints idealize all living creatures because they love them as the creatures of
God and because God loves them.

This tendency of children and of saints to idealize does not make them see things falsely. It
takes the near-sighted or the far-sighted or the
cross-eyed adult to see things wrongly. A moment of disillusionment is enough to make a man
see crooked for weeks, for years, maybe for a life-
time. Perhaps you have verified this observation
in your own experience. If a trusted friend has
failed you, you have perhaps scorned friendship
itself, though against your better judgment. Experience is a good teacher only when it does not
make one need mental spectacles in order to see
aright. The beautiful thing in sanctity is that
every disillusioning experience renders the mental
vision clearer and truer and closer to the perfec-
tion of the child's vision, because the disillusioning experience which the saint suffers must needs

become an illuminating experience. When a saint is played false by a friend, the saint sees how beautiful a thing friendship must be, since it can be so debased. A thing that is already mean can not shock us by its debasement. When a saint considers the horror of sin, he sees its full malice only because he knows the glory of virtue. No one else ever saw sin as Christ saw it in the Garden of Gethsemane, because no one else ever had His knowledge and sense of virtue. No one will ever know the full worth of virtue except the God-man who, knowing the malice of sin, went on with His passion to change sinners into virtuous men.

We of to-day have lost to a great extent our horror of sin because, it seems to me, we do not make sufficient effort to become heroically virtuous. Even the most pious of us feel somewhat unfairly treated when we receive an unusually long penance from a priest in confession. One of the most terrifying accounts of the treatment of a sinner is the story of St. Thais the Penitent, whom the holy Abbot Bessarion shut up in a little closed cell to spend the remainder of her life, with her face turned toward the east while she constantly recited the words, "Thou that hast made me, have mercy on me." Such was her punishment, after she had publicly burned her ill-gotten treasures and made public confession of her sins. When, after three long years of this penance, Bessarion released her, because he had learned from a vision vouchsafed to a Franciscan Friar that angels were preparing for her a place of glory in Heaven, he said to her: "God hath not forgiven thee because of thy repentance, but because of the thought which thou hadst, that thou wouldst deliver thyself over unto Christ." Saints see things positively and value them by the standard of virtue rather than by any lesser standard.

A convincing example of the truth that charity covers a multitude of sins is Christ's forgiveness of Magdalen's many sins, not because of her public penance but because she loved much. To deliver oneself over to Christ in the utter abandonment of trustful, self-forgetting love is to disarm His anger against one's sins. It is sad that Luther's slogan, "Sin and sin boldly, but let your faith be stronger than your sin," could not have been "Love and love boldly, for then you will not sin unto death." That perfect example of glorious, unspoiled childlikeness, the Little Flower of Jesus, preaches again and again in her autobiography the doctrine of love too great for sin. She had practically no knowledge of sin from experience, and yet she knew that love is the only fire that can burn sin to ashes of repentance for man and of forgetfulness for God.

There can be no doubt that it was the consuming fire of betrayed love which came from the eyes of Christ to sear the heart of Peter on the most memorable night of the apostle's life, a fire which would not be quenched until the Savior had three times forced Peter to declare his love publicly before those who knew of its betrayal. We know nothing of the first meeting between the Risen Christ and the unhappy man who had denied Him. We do know that Peter ran immediately to the Tomb when he heard of the Resurrection, as a naughty child might run to his mother on her return home, to cry out his grief over his wrongdoing. We know also that Christ asked Peter three times to tell Him that he really did love Him in spite of his threefold denial.

Children who have been trained by love rather than by fear can easily understand how the great sinner can throw himself lovingly on the breast of Christ and by that act of love become a saint. When the loving child sees a tear brought to the eye of its mother by its wrongdoing, its immediate impulse is to throw itself into her arms with cries of love and stern resolves to be a better child from that moment. It can easily understand the saint who acts thus toward God. And it can readily understand, too, how the saint at times fails to keep his resolves.

The lives of the saints are replete with incidents which can be presented to children in story form as interesting and most effective lessons in imitable virtues. I have found this process of extraction a most fascinating one, though my contact with children has been rather through writing for them than through teaching them. Some time ago I published the first of a series of booklets for children presenting the life and virtues of the Little Flower of Jesus. Some of my grown-up friends were long-suffering enough to say that they liked it, but I was waiting for approval from another source. It came in the most satisfying way. One of my Sisters in religion had a letter from a niece of seven years. In the letter was a poem to the Little Flower, prefaced by the statements: "I wrote a poem. This is it." The lines were written after the little girl had read my verses in my booklet and were inspired no doubt by a desire to improve on their poor quality. I grant that her ambition was duly achieved.

The point is, however, not my satisfaction at the dubious compliment but the fact that children like stories of the saints. It is a great pity that there are so few of these stories in our school readers, even in those edited by Catholics. Of course we have in many places the difficulty of having to use the textbooks required by the state. But there is in such instances no law against the use of supplementary readers, and where we have choice we could very easily give our children more of the lives of the saints. In teaching religion to college seniors I have found that even these young women, who are as a rule rather sophisticated, will listen with interest to child stories about saints, and I try to provide a new one for each lesson. If it happens to be apropos of the lesson, it is well; if it has to be dragged in, it is still very well—just so it gets to the students. This policy may not be in accordance with accepted pedagogy, but at least it helps the girls to know the saints, and to become interested in them. Most of our college students, I find, have very few acquaintances among the holy ones of God, the heroes above all whom they should know. Is this because they were not introduced in childhood?

Of all stories in the lives and legends of

saints, the most appealing to children are, I think, those in which animals play a part. The perennial kindness of saints to animals teaches the much-needed lesson of kindness not merely to animals but to unfortunate human beings as well. Children should be taught early in life that cruelty to animals is wrong because it is unreasonable. Children should never be taught incorrect principles, and so they should learn that though animals have no rights to be respected, wanton cruelty to them is unreasonable and therefore sinful. Sentimental motives are not stable. St. Francis was not being sentimental when he said to the red hot iron about to cauterize his eyeballs, "Brother Fire, God made you beautiful and strong and free, I pray you be gentle with me." He was simply saying in the most inspiring poetry that creatures given for our use are good and worthy of respect because of that reason of usefulness. Animals are given for the use of man, not for his abuse. Being creatures of God they deserve reverence for God's sake. To tie two cats' tails together and fling the creatures over a clothesline may tickle the monstrous humor of certain vicious natures, but it is an unreasonable way of getting amusement. I simply cannot understand such a deed, and I shall never forget my childish horror of two boys who did it and then gleefully watched the suffering creatures tear each other to death. Some children seem to be naturally cruel, not only to animals but to one another as well. They need instruction and also powerful example to lead them aright. The saints furnish abundant examples, which the teacher may use to drive home instruction.

Recently, while reading William Caxton's English translation of the *Legenda Aurea,* I again came across the account of the burial of St. Mary of Egypt. It is so quaint that you will enjoy a part of it.

"And after the year passed Zosimus came again to the desert, and he found her dead, and the body ordinately laid as it should be buried. Zosimus began then anon tenderly to weep, and durst not approach nor touch the body, but said to himself: I would gladly bury this holy body if I knew that I should not displease her. And when he was in this thought he saw lying by her head a letter, that said in this manner: Zosimus, bury right here the body of poor Mary and render to the earth his right, and pray to God for me, at whose commandment the second day after I received Him, He called me from this world. Then Zosimus was much glad that he knew the name

of the saint, but he was greatly dismayed how
he might bury the body, for he had nothing for
to delve the earth with. And anon he saw the
earth dolven, and a sepulchre made by a lion
that came thither. And then Zosimus buried
her, and the lion departed debonairly, and Zosimus returned to his abbey and recounted to his
brethren the conversation of this holy woman
Mary."

I do not know just what or how much Caxton
intended in that adverb "debonairly," but I do
know that for me it has in that place the most
delightful connotation. I can easily see Mr. Lion
swaggering elegantly away across the desert,
lacking only a monocle and swagger stick to make
the picture perfect. I observe the insouciant air
of him that says more plainly than words: "Quite
some little trick, don't cha know, to dig out a
sepulcher for a saint, as if I were one of those
silly domestic dogs—quite condescending on the
part of the lord of the desert and all that—but
really I had to help the poor old man out, and,
in fact, I could have done even more than that
if I had had a mind to."

Of course the good translator did not mean to
conjure up such a picture, but he should not have
written a work so admirable that it would endure

till an irreverent mind of the twentieth century could read it and at his "debonairly" giggle outright. Nor is this delightful interpretation a mere result of my own personal wickedness. I have tried that passage on several devout persons, and each of them has laughed liberally at the lion's exodus. It would not be so dangerous to the normal teacher's decorum, I think, to give to the children the version in Challoner's *Lives of the Fathers in the Desert*. "The lion, like a tame lamb, went his way into the remoter parts of the desert." It would, doubtless, be safer for the teacher and easier for the children, both of whom, for entirely different reasons, might find the word "debonairly" a bit disturbing to mental calm.

In gathering the material wherewith to acquaint the children with the lives of the hermits, one would need to select with care, for the reason that these lives are full of extraordinary penances, which might have the effect of frightening the young spirits trained to modern luxury. The gleaning would not be scant, however, for there are numberless charming incidents that would captivate children. There is the raven, for example, which brought a half loaf of bread daily to St. Paul the Hermit, and which, on the occasion of

St. Anthony's visit to him, provided a whole loaf. Then there are also the two lions that came to dig a grave for Paul so that Anthony could bury him.

Any child will be utterly fascinated by the account of the taming of the fierce wolf of Gubbio by St. Francis. Children the world over have taught dogs to "shake hands"; and here is a fierce man-eating wolf "shaking hands" four separate times with St. Francis and so promising that he will be good and quit his disgraceful habit of eating people. The wolf of Little Red Riding Hood is not nearly so engaging, and is, moreover, only a fictitious wolf. Children will naturally have more reverence for the Sign of the Cross when they see St. Francis making it over a savage wolf and thus turning the wolf into a fawning creature that followed at his heels as meekly as a shepherd dog.

There is, too, that lovely story of St. Anthony's sermon to the fishes. How promptly the vivid imagination of the child will array the fishes with the wee ones in front and the big ones in the rear, just as children sit in school so that they can see teacher—and be seen by teacher, undesirable though it be. Even we older people are delighted in finding one monstrous "fish story" that we can really believe. St. Anthony's life is full of appeal to the child mind. Take, for example, that glorious occasion when the Little Jesus came to play with him and caress him. The tears must come in the heart of any one who reads that lovely story of the Child of Heaven coming into the arms of the man with the sinless soul and the believing heart of a child.

The saints can teach children many lessons. They can teach them how to love God and how to love their neighbor. To illustrate every virtue one can find example in the lives of the saints. There simply is no comparison between the story of the saint and the fairy tale; and yet even our Catholic children as a rule know more of the power of a magic wand than of a Cross traced by the hand of a saint. Is this fair to the children? And is it fair to the saints? Saints know the exact meaning of Christ's command that we be as children if we would enter Heaven, as children of trusting love, unfailing confidence, quick repentance, eager amendment, and unquestioning, democratic charity. The saints belong to children. They are little people, little in their towering humility, and so they are among the little ones that crowd the Kingdom of Heaven. We sophis-

XIV. THE LESSON OF
BERNADETTE OF LOURDES

E live in a purse-proud age. We talk glibly of democracy, and yet comparatively few of us judge others by the standard of personal worth. The external trappings of the man receive far more consideration than does his character. Because of our tendency to social misjudgments I am certain that if a vote were taken to determine the consensus of opinion concerning the greatest woman of the past century, lowly Bernadette of Lourdes would receive not even a respectable minority. The size of this minority would, however, depend absolutely on the diffusion of knowledge of Bernadette among those who love the Blessed Virgin Mary. Any one who loves the Queen of Heaven and who knows the story of Bernadette would perforce grant the greatness of this humble peasant girl of Lourdes.

The reasons of Bernadette's greatness are many, and one of the most important of them is her profound humility. Humility was a conspicuous virtue of our Blessed Lady, who so hon-

ored this little French girl. On the occasion of
the Visitation to Elizabeth, the Virgin Mary did
not merely compose poetry when she sang in her
Magnificat: "My soul doth magnify the Lord,
. . . because He hath regarded the humility of
His handmaid." She really announced a cause
and its effect, which were to be repeated often
in ages to come. Every saint is entitled in some
measure to say that God has regarded the humility of His servant; and no saint, perhaps, can say
it with better right than this most favored child
of our Heavenly Queen, Bernadette of Lourdes.
Few of us moderns would select a child so poor,
so illiterate, so unhealthy as Bernadette to do any
task for us, and yet she was chosen by the Queen
of angels and saints to accomplish a mission second
only to that of the apostles. Lourdes is the living contradiction of infidelity. Lourdes gives
daily testimony to the power of God's mother and
the faith of God's children. Lourdes is in many
ways the most remarkable fact in the world to-
day.

The scientific world went on its knees in homage
to Madame Curie, because of the benefits con-
ferred on mankind by her discovery of radium.
Many are grateful to her for cure of cancer or
other diseases through the radium treatments. But

what homage is not due to the little peasant girl
who, at the bidding of our Lady, scratched the
earth with her hand to release a stream of water
which is to flow always for the instant healing of
thousands diseased in body and soul and for the
benediction and conversion of an unbelieving multitude! The achievement of this child in the face
of tremendous opposition is something to shake
the foundations of incredulity, to awaken the admiration of the mightiest of the mighty, and to
startle the ramparts of materialistic reasoning.
This achievement is tremendous; and yet it was
made humanly possible in consequence of her
humble simplicity. This simplicity, in itself of
course a result of grace, seems to have been more
effective than were the first miracles at Lourdes
in defeating those who opposed Bernadette's mission. By her guilelessness and unfaltering adher-
ence to truth she refuted the arguments of savants
who sought to trap her. By her simple uncon-
cern as she walked in the midst of thousands,
some of whom doubted her sanity, some of whom
worshiped her as one favored of God, others of
whom despised her as an impostor, she proved
unmistakably the divinity of her mission.

There is no more dramatic event in modern
history than the one which occurred on Thursday,

February 11, 1858, an event which was to teach the world the power of the Mother of God. This event occurred near the town of Lourdes in France on the bank of the river Gave, and its immediate setting was Massabielle, which in the simple *patois* of the countryside means "Old Rocks." On that day High Heaven looked down on a scene, the most glorious scene of many centuries. There were two persons in this scene, and they were surrounded by a wild and solitary setting. A mill stream tumbled and frothed over its stony bed till it lost itself in the more placid river, shortly after it had passed the rocks of Massabielle. Just where these huge rocks reared their sullen heads highest into the air, three irregular caverns pierced their structure. The largest cavern was at the base and the two smaller ones were superimposed on this cavern. The three caverns were joined by canals. At the base of the larger of the two upper caverns a wild rose trailed itself along the rock

Kneeling on the bank of the churning stream was a little peasant girl of fourteen years, clad in a patched black dress, with a white *capulet* or mantle covering her head and falling back over her shoulders. On her little feet she wore the coarse *sabots* and stockings of the peasant. Be-

tween her clasped hands was a rosary, the beads
of which were slipped along as she prayed.   Her
delicate face was transfigured.   Her wide brown
eyes glowed with unearthly light as they gazed at
the other person in the scene.

In the larger of the upper caverns of the rock,
with her feet just above the trailing rose, stood
the most beautiful of women, the Virgin Mary.
Ineffable light floated about her—not the glaring
light of the sun but the cool radiance of the morning star.   She was of medium height, of human
flesh like ours, but flesh lustrous, beautiful beyond dreams.   Graceful in immortal youth she
stood.   On her face could be read the innocence
of childhood, the purity of young virginity, the
tender seriousness of motherhood, the wisdom of
ages, all in sweet harmony.   Her robe, long and
graceful, was woven of some unimaginable fabric.
It fell in folds of light to the small white feet
on the dark rock.   On each foot was a golden
rose from which streamed a mystic light.   A wide
blue girdle around her slender waist was knotted
loosely in front and fell to the edge of her robe.
On her head was a white mantle which hovered
like a moon-kissed cloud over her slim virginal
shoulders.   In her clasped hands was a milk-white
rosary, the beads of which were slipped through

her fingers as the little girl before her prayed. She wore no jewels, no diadem; and yet in the blessing of her smile and in the enraptured eyes of the little girl could be read the full measure of this peerless Woman's queenliness over Heaven and earth. The sum of all earthly beauty stood graciously in that little niche in the rock, and High Heaven hovered about the ragged child into whose eyes the Queen of Heaven was smiling.

Why were there in this glorious picture two such contrasting figures? We, in our poor foolish way, would have sought the world over to find a beautiful, cultured woman to represent us on the occasion of Mary's visit to France. We would have furnished a palace for her entertainment, and a thousand ladies-in-waiting. Why did our Lady come to this child in this out-of-the-way place? The answer to this question furnishes the reason of the greatness of Bernadette. Our Lady chose Bernadette for the very same reasons, albeit in lesser measure, as those which brought the angel Gabriel to Mary herself, her innocence and her humility.

Eighteen times did our Lady come from Heaven to stand there in that cavern in the rock and to hold communion with the little girl who could not write or read. Every time she came a larger throng of people were in waiting. They could not see Mary, but they were well content to gaze on the enraptured face of the child who was privileged to converse with her. Monsieur Estrade, who went to Lourdes, as he said, to laugh and enjoy himself thoroughly, "expecting to see a kind of farce or some grotesque absurdities and wondering at the simplicity of so many blockheads," had, after a few minutes' contemplation of the child in ecstasy, "the certitude, the irresistible intuition that a mysterious being was there."

Thousands of eager eyes watched Bernadette when, during the ninth apparition on February 25, she opened the earth for the miraculous fountain of Lourdes, an event which has been and still is of such tremendous consequence. The little girl was entrusted, at the beginning of this apparition, with the third of her secrets. After she had learned this secret there was a brief silence on the part of our Lady. Then her lovely voice again ravished Bernadette's ears.

"Go and drink from the fountain and wash yourself in it and eat of the herb which is growing at its side."

At the word "fountain" Bernadette gazed about her in bewilderment. There was no fountain and there had never been one near the Grotto. She got up from her knees and walked toward the river, but she was stopped by a word from our Lady.

"Do not go there," said Mary, "I have not spoken of drinking from the Gave. Go to the fountain. It is here."

She pointed toward the parched corner of the Grotto, to which, on the preceding morning, she had made Bernadette ascend on her knees. The little girl climbed again to it on her knees. Then, perhaps at some sign from her Queen, she scratched the earth and scooped out a handful. Immediately the hole was filled with water. Bernadette three times lifted the muddy water to her lips in the hollow of her hand before she could force herself to swallow it. Finally she did so, and then bathed her face in the water. She then ate a blade of grass growing beside the hole. Suddenly the water leaped over the brim of the hole and flowed like a thread of silver toward the curious crowd below. At the same moment our Lady disappeared. Bernadette turned to face the crowd. There were streaks of mud on her face. Some of the people jeered. Some cried pitifully: "Bernadette is no longer herself; the poor child has gone mad." Most of them, however, bowed in admiration to the little girl who passed modestly through the crowd and went home.

After the vision and Bernadette's departure, the people examined the ground. It was dry all about, except in the place where Bernadette had dug it with her hand. There the tiny streamlet trickled in increasing volume. To-day the output of water from that fountain is eighteen gallons a minute. Thus came the miraculous water which has given sight to the blind, hearing to the deaf, health to the sick, hope to the hopeless, courage to the despairing, and faith to the unbelieving. The waters of Lourdes have carried their healing power to the four corners of the earth. Little Bernadette drank of them often, but they never brought her physical health. She was chosen for the high favor of suffering, as the Son of Mary singles out His special friends who are brave enough to become martyrs for His sake. Little Bernadette was told by our Lady that she should receive her happiness only when she should come to Heaven. Bernadette understood our Lady well. Eyes that have looked on Mary can never be satisfied with the joys of earth. A heart that loves Mary is glad to suffer for her Son.

On April 4, 1864, the first of the processions at Lourdes was held, in accordance with our

Lady's command given through Bernadette to the Church officials. About fifty thousand persons marched in this procession, people from every walk of life. It was a magnificent demonstration, a triumphal ceremony which marked the close of innumerable difficulties on the part of Bernadette and of those who believed in her mission. The name of the favored child was acclaimed by the multitude, and her story was told from pulpits near and far. The Queen of Heaven, however, feared for the humility of her little handmaid, and so Bernadette was not present to witness her dream come true. Instead, she lay on the humble pallet of public charity in the hospital, her frail body wracked with pain.

The story of Bernadette did not end with the eighteenth apparition of our Lady; it is a continued story whose full meaning will never be known in this world. Three secrets were entrusted to her by our Lady. They were not revealed in the succeeding years during which she lived her simple and laborious life as the daughter of a peasant. They were not revealed in the years during which she lived as a Sister of Charity, serving well the poor and sick. They were not revealed in the thirty years in which her body lay incorrupt in its humble tomb. They were not revealed when that body was given again to the veneration of the public. They were not revealed when the Church hailed her Blessed. The full measure of Bernadette's greatness may, perhaps, be hidden in those secrets. She doubtless prefers it so, because she suffered much when forced to receive adulation. It is the way of those who receive gifts from an earthly sovereign to boast of them. Those who receive gifts from God, however, are prone to hide them in the depths of their own humility.

When Sister Mary Bernard, as Bernadette was called in religion, was once asked whether she did not sometimes feel the temptation to self-esteem in having been thus honored by Mary, she answered: "What a strange idea you have of me! As if I did not know that if the Holy Virgin made choice of me it was because I was the most ignorant of creatures. If she could have discovered another more ignorant she would have chosen her in my place." On another occasion she said that our Lady made use of her just as a woman makes use of a broom. After the woman sweeps she puts the broom into a corner. So, too, said Bernadette: "Our Blessed Lady made use of me, and when my work was done she put me away in a corner. It is the proper place for me. I am happy in it and there I shall stay."

Bernadette did indeed stay in her corner. Her efforts to avoid those who sought her that they might pay her homage were at times almost laughable. No pompous person ever made more heroic efforts to be in the foreground than this humble Sister made to keep herself in the background. She was conspicuous only by her unfailing charity, touching many of the sick unto healing. She who so studiously avoided interviews with persons of wealth or of rank was happy when the sick clamored for her attentions. Bernadette's sense of values had been perfected by that loveliest of women, who stood on a bleak rock and spoke these heart-stirring words, "I am the Immaculate Conception."

This, then, is the lesson of Bernadette—the lesson of humility. Humility is the truth that sees things as they are and measures their values correctly. The lesson of clear-sighted humility is needed to-day more than any other lesson; and it is a lesson that Bernadette is perhaps better qualified than any one else to teach. Humility is the safeguard of innocence, a quality of soul so much endangered by the false standards of to-day. It should be the prayer of us who know

Bernadette that she may intercede for the sin-darkened world, that her glorified hands, no longer limited by time or space, may scoop up the healing waters which once flowed at her touch and scatter them in benediction over the nations. Wherever these drops of water fall, there will surely spring up the flowers of humility and purity and faith.

XV. THE PASSING OF A VALIANT WOMAN

ANY years ago, before the family sitting room threatened to become an obsolete institution, some modest little books appeared under the title *Family Sitting-Room Series*. In one of these books is a sentence which those of us who were friends of the author, Katherine Eleanor Conway, must, now that she has left us, sorrowfully and yet, as always, gratefully apply to her.

"It sometimes happens that a woman may have one friend or several who come to her with the respect, affection, and confidence with which they would approach a cherished, sister; while she, in turn, is perfectly easy and devoid of self-consciousness in their society, rejoices disinterestedly in their successes, sympathizes with their troubles, and out of a heart and mind unvexed by fears of loss or desire of possession, counsels, comforts, and uplifts; or, as need arises, gives reciprocal confidence and seeks reciprocal counsel."

Long before Miss Conway wrote this book, *Making Friends and Keeping Them,* she had learned both the theory and the practice of her art. Many friends there are to mourn the kind, loyal, valiant woman who, on January 4, 1927, was laid to rest in the habit of the Third Order of St. Francis. With the same big generosity of spirit that sent the young Assisian scampering through the streets after a beggar to load the astonished man with money, Miss Conway scattered her bounty to the poor when times were prosperous for her, and, when they were not, she gave her mite as did the widow in the Gospel.

The bounty of Miss Conway was manifested not only in the giving of material gifts but also in the giving of the more precious gifts of mind and heart. I wish I knew how many writers there are in America who can say as I can that never one line of theirs braved the public eye without its word of commendation or of gentle criticism from the gallant little woman in Boston. From her citadel of pain—for during these last nine years her body was twisted out of human semblance by a most agonizing disease of the bone—she kept watch over literary ventures and sent out her message of loving encouragement with an exact intuition for its need.

Those who knew Miss Conway must agree with a characterization of her by John Boyle O'Reilly,

who discovered her genius for the world. "She
is a poet and a logician; she has the heart of a
woman and the brain of a man." Her character
is a rare combination "of strength and tenderness,
of wide, clear intellectual comprehension and of
a poetic and deeply spiritual temperament." She
was artistic without being temperamental in the
wearing sense of the term. She was a woman who
bore many griefs but who never acquired a griev-
ance. She used to say that she had no sense of
humor, but those who met her during her long
years of suffering found that it had developed
with adversity. Her bravery in the face of constant pain had certainly something of the laughter
of saints in it, for it was an understanding bravery
that looked across the misted years into the glory
of light beyond. Surely at the end of her street
there are stars and sunrise and glory of rest in
peace.

Miss Conway was often asked by her friends
the rebellious question, "Why must *you* bear all
this pain?" And her answer—such a complete,
satisfying answer to the person of faith—was invariably, "God and my confessor know." If not
for her sins, as we who love her like to think,
then for the sins of the world, pain was a trifling
price for her to pay that they might be atoned for

with some slight measure of justice. The world needs the slow martyrdom of brave ones like her to weigh in the balance with itself against Divine Justice. God manifested one of His exquisite thoughtfulnesses toward those who will allow themselves to become His chosen friends when He called her to Himself on the beautiful Feast of the Most Holy Name. She had an adoring devotion to the Sacred Name of Our Savior, which she satisfied daily by reading the Psalms that hymn the praises of the Name of Jesus.

Katherine Eleanor Conway was born in Rochester, New York, on September 6, 1852. She wrote her first poem at the age of fifteen. She began her literary and journalistic career on the Rochester *Daily Union and Advertiser.* The attention of Boston was first attracted to her when she wrote the poem "Remember" and submitted it to John Boyle O'Reilly, editor of the *Pilot.* Mr. O'Reilly recognized her talent and engaged her to work on his staff. From 1883 to 1908 she served as associate editor of the *Pilot.* Miss Conway was for several years a member of the editorial staff of the *Boston Republic.*

Miss Conway's fame was gradually spreading. In 1907 she was awarded the Laetare medal, given annually by the University of Notre Dame

to some member of the Catholic laity for service
to religion, art, science, philanthropy, or other
public work. In 1912 the attention of the Catholic world was directed toward her. Pope Pius X
bestowed the *Pro Ecclesia et Pontifice* medal upon
her for distinguished services to the Church.
Few women have received such recognition. Miss
Conway was at this time a professor of English
literature and of Church history at St. Mary's
College, Notre Dame, Indiana. With delegations
from all over the nation and the entire student
body in proud attendance, Miss Conway was
awarded the medal, which had been brought from
Rome by the late Very Reverend Andrew Mor-
rissey, C.S.C., D.D., then Provincial of the Order
of the Holy Cross in America. Accompanying the
medal was a diploma signed by His Eminence
Cardinal Merry del Val and a photograph of
Pope Pius X with an autographed message.

Of Miss Conway's years at St. Mary's, from
1911 to 1915, it is difficult for me to say anything.
The joys of remembering them are too much akin
to pain just now. Her little room was a gathering place for literary aspirants, of course, but it
was more than that; it was a gathering place
of friends. Despite the fact that she protested
a lack of humor, many little half-forgotten

laughs lurk in the corners of that room.
There was the day, for example, when I happened
into the room to find her without her glasses,
which was almost like finding her *en déshabille*
in that room. She chuckled a bit when I came
close to her and then uttered this dubious compliment, "I should like to go without my glasses
all the time, for I saw you surrounded by a rosy
mist which made you really beautiful."

Miss Conway was intensely religious. She had
a keen understanding of the purpose of human
life and the necessity of every one's discovering
and following the particular vocation offered one
by God. Only those who knew her could realize
how fully she understood her own vocation of
literary leadership among Catholics. Her appreciation of the life of the religious was entire
and beautiful. On the occasion of my religious
profession, which occurred after she had found
it necessary to leave St. Mary's because of her
failing health, she wrote me a letter, which is so
characteristic of this appreciation and of her own
lovely inner life as to justify quotation here.

"What shall I say to you on this best day of
all your earthly days! If I were near you, I
could touch your hand and look at you; and you
would know what is in my heart for you. I have

thought of you very often since last May. Perhaps I was getting ever so faintly the sound of the approaching footsteps of the Beautiful One in His robe, walking in the greatness of His strength, to make you His own in the surest way forever. Oh, to-day, when your word is so powerful with Him, crowd in just one little petition for me! I join my congratulations to those of the dear ones with you to-day. Look for a long letter from me when I am a bit stronger."

Many long letters came in the years from that time till her death, though she did not become "a bit stronger." Neither of us suspected then the *via dolorosa* that she must tread before she heard the footsteps of the Beautiful One coming to take her to be His own forever.

Miss Conway was the daughter of cultured Catholic parents who came to this country from the west of Ireland. Upon her mother's side are traditions of scholarship for many generations, several of her kinsmen having been prominent ecclesiastics. The name is of remote Welsh origin and there is a slight trace of English in the family, but they gloried in their Irish blood. Miss Conway was educated by the Religious of the Sacred Heart in Rochester and at St. Mary's Academy, Buffalo, New York, where her inclinations to literature were strengthened by a gifted teacher. Her busy mind was ever instinctively reaching out toward wider activities, and she found an able assistant in her friend and adviser, Bishop McQuaid of Rochester, New York. She edited for five years the *West End Journal,* a religious monthly. From 1880-1883 she was assistant editor of the *Catholic Union and Times.*

Miss Conway was founder of the John Boyle O'Reilly Reading Circle and was for more than eighteen years its president. She was a member of the New England Women's Press Association, the Boston Author's Club, the League of Catholic Women, the Ladies' Catholic Benevolent Association, and the Children of Mary. She was known in Boston for her charitable works as well as for her literary ones.

The literary output of Miss Conway's fine, energetic genius is one of which the Catholic world may well be proud. Two of her best-known works are a novel, *Lalor's Maples,* and her *Watchwords from John Boyle O'Reilly.* It is sad that her editorial articles must share the fate of their kind, and yet, since they served their timely purpose, we must let them be forgotten as are all voices that cry in the wilderness, once the wilderness has been penetrated by friend and foe alike. Her book of poems, *A Dream of Lilies,* aroused expectations which were amply fulfilled. Another volume of poems was in preparation for publication when the author's tireless hands were stilled by death, and it has since been published under the title *The Color of Life.*

Miss Conway's works abide a living monument to her. We are grateful that so much has been left to us. There is always a wistful note of otherworldliness in her writings, as there was always a vision of Heaven in her eyes.

(1)

THE END